MILITARY OPERATIONS OF THE FALKLANDS WAR

Books LLC®, Wiki Series, Memphis, USA, 2011. ISBN: 9781156679593. www.booksllc.net
Copyright: http://creativecommons.org/licenses/by-sa/3.0/deed.en

Table of Contents

Battles of the Falklands War
Battle of Goose Green 1
Battle of Mount Harriet 4
Battle of Mount Longdon 6
Battle of Mount Tumbledown 11
Battle of San Carlos (1982) 13
Battle of Seal Cove 17
Battle of Two Sisters 18
Battle of Wireless Ridge 20

Bluff Cove Air Attacks 22
Mount Kent Skirmish 23
Raid on Pebble Island 23
Skirmish at Many Branch Point 24
Skirmish at Top Malo House 25

Military operations of the Falklands War
1982 invasion of the Falkland Islands 26
Invasion of South Georgia 31
Operation Algeciras 34
Operation Black Buck 37
Operation Corporate 41
Operation Keyhole 41
Operation Mikado 42
Operation Paraquet 42
Operation Sutton 43

Introduction

Purchase of this book entitles you to a free trial membership in the publisher's book club at www.booksllc.net. (Time limited offer.) Simply enter the barcode number from the back cover onto the membership form. The book club entitles you to select from hundreds of thousands of books at no additional charge. You can also download a digital copy of this and related books to read on the go. Simply enter the title or subject onto the search form to find them.

Each chapter in this book ends with a URL to a hyperlinked online version. Type the URL exactly as it appears. If you change the URL's capitalization it won't work. Use the online version to access related pages, websites, footnotes, tables, color photos, updates. Click the version history tab to see the chapter's contributors. Click the edit link to suggest changes.

A large and diverse editor base collaboratively wrote the book, not a single author. After a long process of discussion and debate, the chapters gradually took on a neutral point of view reached through consensus. Additional editors expanded and contributed to chapters striving to achieve balance and comprehensive coverage. This reduced the regional or cultural bias found in many other books and provided access and breadth on subject matter otherwise little documented.

Battle of Goose Green

The **Battle of Goose Green** (28–29 May 1982) was an engagement of the Falklands War between British and Argentine forces. Goose Green and its neighbour Darwin are settlements on East Falkland in the Falkland Islands. They lie on Choiseul Sound on the east side of the island's central isthmus. They are about 13 miles south of the site of the major British amphibious landings in San Carlos Water (Operation Sutton).

The bulk of the Argentine forces were in positions around Port Stanley about 50 miles (80 km) to the east of San Carlos. The position at Goose Green and Darwin was well defended by a force of combined units totalling about 1,200 (at the start of the battle the number was thought to be less than half this), well equipped with artillery, mortars, 30 mm cannon and machine guns. However the force was fairly static and judged to present little threat to the bridgehead. Consequently it had no strategic military value for the British in their campaign to recapture the islands, so early plans for land operations had called for Goose Green to be isolated and bypassed.

Things changed in the days following the landings on 21 May. While the bridgehead was being consolidated no offensive ground operations of any size were feasible and yet Argentine air attacks caused significant loss of and damage to British ships in the sea area around the landing grounds. This led to a feeling among senior commanders and politicians in the UK that the momentum of the campaign was being lost.

As a result British Joint Headquarters in the UK came under increasing pressure from the British government for an early ground offensive. And so, on the 25th May Brigadier Julian Thompson, ground forces commander, commanding 3 Commando Brigade was ordered to mount an attack on Argentine positions around Goose Green and Darwin.

Prelude

Italo Piaggi, Argentine commander, c. 1982

The British force consisted of three rifle companies, one patrol company, one support company, and the HQ company of Lieutenant-Colonel Herbert 'H' Jones' 2nd Battalion the Parachute Regiment (2 Para) which had the following support: three 105 mm artillery pieces with 960 shells from 29 Commando Regiment, Royal Artillery; one MILAN anti-tank missile platoon; Scout helicopters, and at dusk, air support was provided by three Royal Air Force Harriers later in the battle. HMS *Arrow* shelled the Argentine forward positions. Lieutenant-Colonel Jones commanded the battalion.

The defending Argentine forces known as Task Force Mercedes consisted of the Lieutenant-Colonel Italo Piaggi's 12th Infantry Regiment (RI 12) and a company of the Ranger-type 25th Infantry Regiment (Argentina) (RI 25). Lieutenant-Colonel Mohamed Alí Seineldín, considered by many Argentines to be the 'father' of the Argentine commandos, who chafing at his role as commanding officer of an ordinary infantry unit, put all his conscripts through a compressed version of the commando course in March 1982, dressing them in the green berets of the Army Commandos and changing the title of RI 25 unofficially to 25th 'Special' Infantry Regiment.

Air defence was provided by a battery of six 20 mm Rheinmetall manned by Air Force personnel and two radar-guided Oerlikon 35 mm anti-aircraft guns from the 601st Anti-Aircraft Battalion that would be employed in a ground support role in the last stages of the fighting. There was also one battery of four 105 mm Oto Melara pack howitzers from the 4th Airborne Artillery Regiment. Pucarás based at Stanley, armed with rockets and napalm, provided ground support. Unbeknownst to the Argentine outpost, a four-man SAS patrol, commanded by Corporal Trevor Brookes, had infiltrated the 12th Regiment's A Company area, attempting to pinpoint the Argentinian positions. Brookes successfully avoided, for over a fortnight, Argentine helicopter and foot patrols sent to find them.

Battle

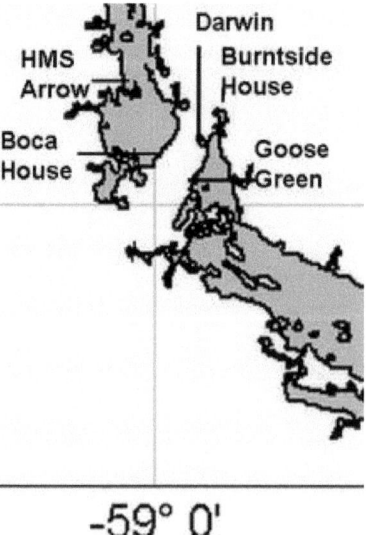

Detailed map of Goose Green isthmus.

Just after 2.30 am of May 28, 2nd Para launched its attack on the Argentines to capture Goose Green 'before breakfast'. RI 12's A Company defended the Darwin Parks sector with two rifle platoons, and a mortar platoon. For 90 minutes the forward Argentine platoons were pounded with naval artillery from HMS *Arrow*. In the ensuing night battle about twelve Argentines were killed. The platoon under Sub-Lieutenant Malacalza fought a delaying action against the British paratroopers, blooding themselves on Burntside Hill before taking up combat positions again on Darwin Ridge. Major Philip Neame's D Company was temporarily halted by the Coronation Ridge position. One of his men, Lance-Corporal Gary Bingley darted out from under cover to charge the enemy machine gun nest that was holding up the advance. He was hit 10 metres (11 yd) from the machine gun, but shot two of the crew before collapsing. He was posthumously awarded the Military Medal. With the enemy machine gun out of action, the Paras were able to clear the Argentine platoon position, but at the cost of three dead.

Then 2nd Para moved on to the south via Darwin Parks. The Argentines made a determined stand along Darwin Ridge. As A and B Companies moved south from Coronation Ridge they were raked by fire from a couple of concealed Argentine FN MAG machine guns. An Argentine senior NCO, Company Sergeant-Major Juan Cohelo, is credited with rallying the RI 12's A Company remnants falling back from Darwin Parks. He was seriously wounded later in the day. The first British assault was broken up by fire from Sub-Lieutenant Ernesto Peluffo's RI 12 platoon. Corporal Osvaldo Olmos, of RI 25 refused to leave his foxhole and continued firing at the British company as it moved forward. The Paras called on the Argentines to surrender.

At this juncture of the battle, 2nd Para's advance had become stuck. A Company was in the gorse line at the bottom of Darwin Hill, and against the entrenched Argentines who were looking down the hill at them. As daylight was now all over the battlefield, Jones led an unsuccessful charge up a small gully resulting in the death of the adjutant, Captain Wood, A company's second-in-command Captain Dent, and Corporal Hardman. Shortly thereafter Jones was seen to run West along the base of Darwin Ridge to a small re-entrant, followed by his bodyguard. He checked his Stirling SMG then ran up the hill toward an Argentine trench. He was seen to be hit once, then fell, then got up and was hit again from the side. He fell metres short of the trench and Jones had been hit in the back and the groin, and died within minutes. Jones was later to receive the Victoria Cross for his efforts. As Jones lay dying, his men radioed for urgent casualty evacuation. However, the British Scout Helicopter sent to evacuate Jones was shot down by an Argentine FMA IA 58 Pucara ground attack aircraft. The pilot, Lt. Richard Nunn RM was killed and posthumously received the DFC, and the aircrewman, Sgt. Belcher RM badly wounded in both legs. Corporal Ríos was later fatally wounded in his trench by Corporal Abols firing a 66 mm rocket.

By then it was 10.30 am and Major Dair Farrar-Hockley's A Company made a third attempt, but this petered out. Eventually the British company, hampered by the morning fog as they advanced up the slope of Darwin Ridge, were driven back to the gulley by the fire of 1st Platoon of RI 25's C Company, under the command of 2nd Lieutenant Roberto Estévez. During this action Lieutenant Estévez directed Argentine 105 mm artillery and 120 mm mortar fire that posthumously earned him the Argentine Nation to the Heroic Valour in Combat Cross (CHVC). 2nd Para's mortar crews fired 1,000 rounds to keep the enemy at bay, and helped stop the Argentines getting a proper aim at the Paras.

It was almost noon before the British advance resumed. Inspired by their commanding officer's sacrifice, A Company soon cleared the eastern end of the Argentine position and opened the way forward. There had been two battles going on in the Darwin hillocks – one around Darwin Hill looking down on Darwin Bay, and an equally fierce one in front of Boca Hill, also known as Boca House Ruins. Sub-Lieutenant Guillermo Aliaga's 3rd Platoon of RI 8's C Company held Boca Hill. The position of Boca Hill was taken after heavy fighting by Major John Crosland's B Company with support from the MILAN anti-tank platoon. Crosland was the most experienced British officer, and as the events of the day unfolded, it was later said that Crosland's cool and calm leadership of his soldiers on the battlefield turned the Boca House section of the front line. About the time of the victory at the Boca Hill position, A Company overcame the Argentine defenders on Darwin Hill, finally taking the position that had caused many casualties on both sides. Majors Farrar-Hockley and Crosland each won the Military Cross for their efforts. Corporal David Abols received a Distinguished Conduct Medal for his daring charges which turned the Darwin Hill battle.

After the victory on Darwin Ridge, C and D Companies began to make their way to the small airfield as well as Darwin School, which was east of the airfield, while B Company made their way south of Goose Green Settlement. A Company remained on Darwin Hill. C company was decimated when they became the target of intense anti-aircraft 35 mm direct fire. They suffered a 20 per cent casualties. Lieutenant James Barry's No. 12 Platoon, D company, saw some fierce action at the airfield. They were ambushed, but one of his men shot dead two of the attackers, and then reported the events to Major Neame. The platoon sergeant charged the attacking enemy with his machine gun, killing four of them. For his bravery Sergeant Wyndham Williams was awarded the Distinguished Conduct Medal. Private Graham Carter won the Military Medal by rallying No. 12 Platoon and leading it forward at bayonet point to take the airfield. The RI 25 platoon defending the airfield fled into the Darwin-Goose Green track and was able to escape. Sergeant Sergio Garcia, of RI 25, single-handedly covered the withdrawal of his platoon during the British counterattack. He was posthumously awarded the Argentine Nation to the Valour in Combat Medal. Four of D Company and approximately a dozen Argentines were killed in these engagements. Among the dead was Lieutenant Barry, who, along with two comrades, was killed while accepting the surrender of a group of Argentines. C Company had not lost a single man in the Darwin School fighting, but a soldier was later killed from a burst of Argentine 35 mm anti-aircraft fire, which reduced the building to rubble.

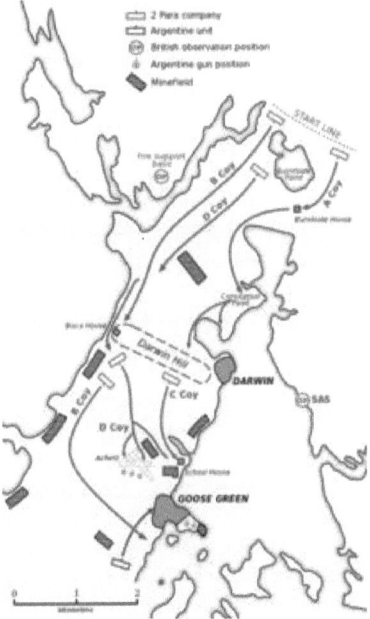

The Battle of Goose Green, 28–29 May 1982

As day became night, two Argentine Air Force warrant officers who were POWs were sent to the Argentine commanders at Goose Green by the acting CO of 2nd Para, Major Chris Keeble, with the terms of surrender.

"MILITARY OPTIONS

We have sent a PW to you under a white flag of truce to convey the following military options:

1. That you unconditionally surrender your force to us by leaving the township, forming up in a military manner, removing your helmets and laying down your weapons. You will give prior notice of this intention by returning the PW under a white flag with him briefed as to the formalities by no later than 0830 hrs local time.

2. You refuse in the first case to surrender and take the inevitable consequences. You will give prior notice of this intention by returning the PW without his flag (although his neutrality will

be respected) no later than 0830 hrs local time.
3. In the event and in accordance with the terms and conditions of the Geneva Convention and Laws of War you will be held responsible for the fate of any civilians in Darwin and Goose Green and we in accordance with these terms do give notice of our intention to bombard Darwin and Goose Green.
C KEEBLE
Commander of British Forces"

'Juliet' Company, 42 Commando (composed mainly of members of Naval Party 8901) was flown to Darwin to reinforce 2 Para and at the same time plans were made that night for 'Bravo' Company, 6th Regiment to be taken by helicopter to Goose Green in a spoiler move.

The following day Lieutenant-Colonel Piaggi surrendered all Argentine forces, approximately 1,000 men, including 202 men of the Air Force. He was later discharged from the army in disgrace. Major Keeble was awarded the Distinguished Service Order. The fourteen-hour battle had cost the British 17 killed and 64 wounded, the majority from 2nd Para. Around 50 Argentines were killed and 120 wounded. After the battle vast quantities of Argentine weapons and unused ammunition were deployed among ships of the Royal Navy still stationed at San Carlos Water.

BBC incident

During the planning of the assault of both Darwin and Goose Green, the Battalion Headquarters were listening in to the BBC World Service. The newsreader announced that the 2nd Battalion of the Parachute Regiment were poised and ready to assault Darwin and Goose Green, causing great confusion with the commanding officers of the battalion. Lieutenant Colonel Jones became furious with the level of incompetence and told BBC representative Robert Fox he was going to sue the BBC, Whitehall and the War Cabinet. The Argentine forces were listening in to the broadcast, just as Jones feared. Doubtless working on the assumption that no country would announce its army's battle plans to the enemy, they dismissed it as a crude bluff. Battalion Headquarters had no way of knowing this and Major Chris Keeble was all for calling off the assault.

Argentine Military Trials of 2009

Argentine army officers and NCOs were later charged with abusing and killing their own troops at Goose Green. "Our own officers were our greatest enemies," says Ernesto Alonso, the president of CECIM, a veterans group founded by Rodolfo Carrizo and other conscripts of the 7th Regiment. "They supplied themselves with whiskey from the pubs, but they weren't prepared for war. "They disappeared when things got serious." There are others who maintain that the conscripts were helped to make themselves as comfortable as possible under the circumstances and that their officers and NCOs fought well and tried hard to bolster morale.

In 2009, Argentine authorities in Comodoro Rivadavia ratified a decision made by authorities in Río Grande, Tierra del Fuego (which, according to Argentina, have authority over the islands) charging 70 officers and NCOs with inhumane treatment of conscript soldiers during the war. "We have testimony from 23 people about a soldier who was shot to death by a corporal, four other former combatants who starved to death, and at least 15 cases of conscripts who were staked out on the ground," Pablo Vassel, under-secretary of human rights in the province of Corrientes, told Inter Press Service News Agency.

On 19 May a 12th Regiment conscript, Secundino Riquelme, reportedly died of starvation. There are claims, however, that false testimonies were used as evidence in accusing the Argentine officers and NCOs of abandonment and Vassel had to step down from his post as under-secretary of human rights of Corrientes in 2010. Other veterans are sceptical about the veracity of the accusations with Colonel Martiniano Duarte saying that it has become "fashionable" for ex-conscripts to now accuse their superiors of abandonment. Former conscript Fernando Cangiano has also dismissed the claims about the "supposed widespread sadism present among the Argentine officers and NCOs" and the claim that the conscripts had not handled themselves well in the fighting. Former conscript César Trejo also accused the current Argentine Ministry of Defense, Nilda Garré of promoting a "state of confused politics" in favour of the CECIM.

Sub-Lieutenant Gustavo Malacalza is accused of having staked three conscripts at Goose Green, for having abandoned their positions to go looking for food and revealing their positions with gunfire. "We said it was going to be us next," said Private Mario Oscar Nuñez recalling the death of conscript Riquelme. Soon after the British landings, he and two other conscripts took the decision to kill a sheep. The three men were skinning the sheep when they were discovered by Sub-Lieutenant Malacalza, who was accompanied by fellow conscripts of A Company, 12th Regiment and given a beating. "They started kicking and stamping on us. Finally came the staking."
Source (edited): "http://en.wikipedia.org/wiki/Battle_of_Goose_Green"

Battle of Mount Harriet

The **Battle of Mount Harriet** was an engagement of the Falklands War, which took place on the night of 11/12 June 1982 between British and Argentine forces. It was one of three battles in a brigade-size operation on the same night.

Forces

The British force consisted of 42 Commando (42 CDO), Royal Marines under the command of Lt. Col. Nick Vaux's

Royal Marines (he later became a general) with artillery support from a battery of 29 Commando Regiment, Royal Artillery. The 1st Battalion, Welsh Guards (1WG) and two companies from 40 CDO were in reserve. HMS *Yarmouth* provided naval-gunfire support for the British forces.

The Argentine defenders consisted of Lieutenant Colonel Diego Soria's 4th Infantry Regiment (RI 4).

Build-up to the battle

On the night of 30 May, K Company of 42 CDO moved forward of San Carlos to secure the commanding heights of Mount Kent—at 1,504 feet, the tallest of the peaks surrounding Stanley—where the D Squadron SAS Troops had already established a strong presence. However, when they arrived at their landing zone, some 3 kilometres (2 mi) behind the ridge of the mountain, the Marines were surprised to see the flashes and lines of tracer ammunition lighting up the night. After a fierce fight at close quarters, the Argentine patrol (Captain Tomas Fernandez' 2nd Assault Section, 602 Commando Company) melted away from the boulders and snow-soaked scrub and grass. By the end of May, Major Cedric Delves' D Squadron had gained Mount Kent, and Tactical HQ commenced patrolling Bluff Cove Peak, which they took with the loss of two wounded.

The attack was preceded by many days of observation and nights of patrolling. Some night-fighting patrols were part of a deception plan to convince the Argentinians that the attack would come from a westerly direction. Other, more covert, patrols were to find a route through a minefield around the south of Mount Harriet. Sniping and naval artillery were used to harass the defenders and deny them sleep.

On 3 June, Lieutenant Chris Marwood's Reconnaissance Troop of 42 CDO, accompanying the 3 Commando Brigade Forward Air Control team commanded by Flight Lieutenant Dennis Marshall-Hasdell, encountered an RI 4 fighting patrol (3rd Platoon of B Company). The Recce Troop opened fire and two conscripts (Privates Celso Paez and Roberto Ledesma) were instantly killed, and an NCO (Corporal Nicolas Odorcic) went down, wounded by a head shot by one of the Marine snipers as he took cover among the rocks. This action drew attention to their exposed forward position, and Argentine reinforcements joined the action with a general counterattack. The Primary Forward Air Controller, commando-trained Flight Lieutenant Dennis Marshal-Hasdell, remembers: "We were separated from our heavy bergens with the radios and all our gear. The patrol was spread over quite a large area, with lots of shouting, noise and firing going on. The Marines abandoned all their equipment, and although no one told us, it became clear that we were to withdraw. With no information, and the likelihood of having to fight our way out, Dave Greedus and I decided to abandon our equipment, destroying as much as we could. The two radio sets (HF and UHF) were tough enough, but the HAZE unit of the laser target marker was designed to withstand the weight of a tank!"

The Laser Target Designator retrieved in the contact showed that the Royal Marines were seeking to destroy the Argentine bunkers on Mount Harriet with 1,000-pound Pave Way Laser Guided Bombs.

On the night of 8-9 June, action on the outer defence zone flared when Lieutenant Mark Townsend's 1 Troop (K Company, 42 CDO) probed Mount Harriet, killing two Argentines. At the same time, two platoon-size fighting patrols from 45 Commando attempted the same on Two Sisters Mountain, but the Argentine Rasit ground surveillance radar there was able to detect the 45 Commando platoons, and artillery fire dispersed the force.

Over a period of a week, the 4th Regiment defended the Harriet-Two Sisters sector from five Royal Marine platoon-size attacks. Every time the Royal Marine Commandos got into the forward platoon positions, the officers, NCOs and conscripts, counterattacked with rifles and cleared them out.

On the morning of 11 June, the orders for the attack were given to 42 CDO by Vaux; K Company was ordered to attack the eastern end of the mountain, while L Company would attack the southern side an hour later, where it—if the mountain was secured—would then move north of Mount Harriet to Goat Ridge. J Company would launch a diversionary attack (code named Vesuvius) on the western end of Mount Harriet.

In the closing hours of 11 June, K and L Companies moved from their assembly area on Mount Challenger (which lay to the west of Mount Harriet) and made their way south, around their objective, across the minefield, to their respective start lines. As they moved around the feature in the dark, J company launched their very loud diversionary "attack" from the west.

Battle Summary

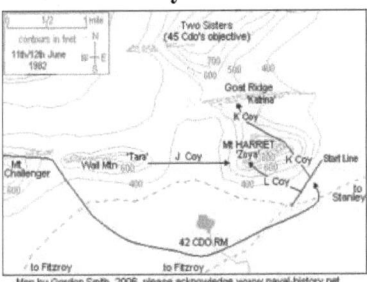

Map by Gordon Smith, 2006, please acknowledge www.naval-history.net

The battle for Mount Harriet began on the evening of 11 June with a blistering naval bombardment that killed two Argentines and wounded twenty-five. John Witheroe, one of the British war correspondents, later recalled the softening up fire:

"We were involved with one night attack on Mount Harriet, when the Welsh Guards were coming up as a back-up. This involved marching for several hours on a very dark night, through a minefield. Sporadic shellfire slowed our progress tremendously. Eventually we made the base of Mount Harriet, which was coming under incredible fire from a frigate off shore. The whole mountain seemed to erupt in flame. It seemed impossible that anybody could survive an attack like that. This went on for well over an hour, shell after shell whistling over our heads and hitting the mountain. Eventually this was lifted and the Marines went in. To our amazement, there seemed to be an incredible amount of fighting going on. There was a lot of tracer fire. The whole night was being lit up by flares, which cast a dead, unrealistic, pall over the whole scene.

Captain Peter Babbington's K Company crossed their start line first and proceeded up the mountain undetected, knifing two sentries on the way. They remained undetected until they approached Sub-Lieutenant Mario Juarez' 120-mm Mortar Platoon positions and decided to engage them. They were assisted in the advance by HMS *Yarmouth*, artillery, and mortars. During the engagement, Corporal Larry Watts was killed. About 150 metres from Soria's HQ, Corporal Steve Newland circled behind a group of Argentines (under First Lieutenant Jorge Alejandro Echeverria, the 4th Regiment's intelligence officer) who were setting up an ambush. Although half a dozen Argentines and a MAG were placed to engage anyone who broke cover, Newland darted out from under cover to charge the enemy machine gun. He grenaded two of the crew, but reaching the rear of the machine gun position, he was shot through both legs. With the enemy machine gun out of action, Corporals Mick Eccles and Sharky Ward were able to clear the position with some help from Marine Lingard. The three corporals were awarded the Military Medal. Increasing numbers of Argentine soldiers, mainly conscripts from RI 4's Recce Platoon, began to surrender, but the Commanding Officer and Intelligence Officer and several senior NCOs still fought on, according to their orders. The heavy machine gun teams, to a man, stood in their positions continuing the fight.

L Company crossed their start line shortly after K Company and were almost immediately engaged by effective machine gun fire from Sub-Lieutenant Pablo Oliva's platoon defending the lower southern slopes. These weapons would not be silenced until being hit by several MILAN anti-tank missiles and six 105mm artillery guns from Mount Challenger. The L Company Marines contend they took fire from at least seven machine guns that wounded five men, including the company's second-in-command and a signaller. Hugh Bicheno contends that the 4th Regiment's passive night goggles were all with B Company.

Before first light, Lieutenant Jerry Burnell's 5 Troop of L Company proceeded to an outcrop of rocks towards Goat Ridge. As they advanced, the Royal Marine platoon came under heavy fire from a 16-men machine-gun team of grenadiers from the *Regimiento de Granaderos a Caballo del General San Martín* covering the Argentinian retreat and were forced to withdraw under cover of machine guns pre-positioned behind them and further up the hill. The Troop took one casualty in this action. L Company requested mortar fire onto the Argentines; a mixture of HE and WP; then 5 Troop moved forward again. They took 3 prisoners although most of the *granaderos* had withdrawn, along with two rifle platoons. Further fighting went on throughout the morning of 12 June, including a conscript, in a position just below the summit, who held up L Company with accurate shooting until killed by an 84mm anti-tank rocket fired at short range.

Aftermath

The battle was a textbook example of good planning and use of deception and surprise, and a further step towards their main objective of Stanley. Two British soldiers: Corporal Larry Watts and Acting Corporal J. Smith were killed, and twenty-six were wounded. Eighteen Argentine dead lay around the defences. Lance Corporal Koleszar had the surprising experience of finding that two 'dead' Argentine soldiers, whose boots he was trying to remove, were very much alive and jumped up to surrender. Some British reporters were thus misled into depicting the Argentinians as hapless teenage conscripts who caved in after the first shots were fired, but Royal Marine Warrant Officer 2 John Cartledge, who served with L Company during the battle, corrected them, saying the Argentines were good soldiers who had fought properly:

"They used the tactics which they had been taught along the way very well, they were quite prepared for an attack. They put up a strong fight from start to finish. They were also better equipped than we were. We had first generation night sights, which were large cumbersome pieces of equipment, while the Argentines had second-generation American night sights that were compact and so much better than what we had. The one deficiency which we exposed was that they had planned for a western end of the mountain attack and therefore had not bothered to extend their defensive positions to the eastern end, where we ultimately attacked."

One British general put their success down to his Marines' skill and professionalism:

"What was needed was speed but not being bloody stupid. The Israelis would have done it much faster, but with many more casualties."

42 Commando captured 300 prisoners on Mount Harriet, and for the bravery shown in the attack, the unit was awarded one DSO, one Military Cross, four Military Medals, and eight men were mentioned in dispatches.

Source (edited): "http://en.wikipedia.org/wiki/Battle_of_Mount_Harriet"

Battle of Mount Longdon

The **Battle of Mount Longdon** was an engagement of the Falklands War between British and Argentine forces, which took place on 11–12 June 1982, resulting in the British victory and their occupation of a key position around the besieged Argentine garrison.

Background

British forces

The British force consisted of 3 PARA under Lieutenant Colonel Hew Pike (later general) with artillery support from six 105 mm light guns of 29 Commando Regiment, Royal Artillery; 2 PARA were in reserve. Naval gunfire support was provided by HMS Avenger's 4.5-in gun.

Argentine forces

The Argentine force consisted of B Company of the 7th Infantry Regiment (RI 7), as well as other detachments from other units. The local Argentine commander was Major Carlos Carrizo-Salvadores, the second-in-command of RI 7. The 7th Infantry Regiment, reinforced by two of the Marine Infantry platoons, held Mount Longdon, Wireless Ridge and Cortley Ridge to the east. Marine Sub-Lieutenant (naval rank equivalent to captain) Sergio Dachary had arrived on Mount Longdon in the week preceding the battle, and was on hand to control the Marine-manned heavy machine-guns on Mount Longdon.

Mostly conscripts with a year of training, the young RI 7 soldiers were not going to rout the field easily and most were prepared to stand their ground. They possessed fully automatic FN FAL rifles which delivered more firepower than the British SLR, FN MAG 7.62mm general purpose machineguns identical to those of the Paras; some fifty of the 7th Regiment were to fight more resolutely than the rest, having been trained on a commando course organized by commando-trained Major Oscar Jaimet, the Operations Officer of the 6th Infantry Regiment (RI 6). Private Jorge Altieri, in an interview after the war told how he trained hard with B Company:

I was issued with a FAL 7.62 millimetre rifle. Other guys were given FAPs – light machineguns – and others got PAMS [submachineguns]. The main emphasis in shooting was making every bullet count. I was also shown how to use a bazooka, how to make and lay booby-traps, and how to navigate at night, and we went on helicopter drills, night and day attacks and ambushes.

He also maintains that lentils, green peas and a bit of mutton constituted the main meals that were served between 16th April and 11th June but these meals were supplemented by a few luxuries such as chocolate bars and pre-packaged combat rations. However, in Altieri's own words

No estábamos bien alimentados previo a los combates como debe ser, estábamos debilitados. (We were undernourished before the battle, we were weakened).

Sub-Lieutenant Juan Domingo Baldini is accused of having staked several conscripts for having abandoned their posts to go looking for food, an act punishable by death in other armies. "Our own officers were our greatest enemies," says Ernesto Alonso, the president of CECIM, a veterans group founded by Rodolfo Carrizo and former conscripts of the 7th Regiment. "They supplied themselves with whiskey from the pubs, but they weren't prepared for war. They disappeared when things got serious." There are others who maintain that these men were helped to make themselves as comfortable as possible under the circumstances and that their officers tried hard to bolster morale. In 2009, Argentine authorities in Comodoro Rivadavia ratified a decision made by authorities in Río Grande, Tierra del Fuego (which, according to Argentina, have authority over the islands) charging 70 officers and NCOs with inhumane treatment of conscript soldiers during the war. "We have testimony from 23 people about a soldier who was shot to death by a corporal, four other former combatants who starved to death, and at least 15 cases of conscripts who were staked out on the ground," Pablo Vassel, under-secretary of human rights in the province of Corrientes, told Inter Press Service News Agency. There are claims that false testimonies were used as evidence in accusing the Argentine officers and NCOs and Vassel had to step down from his post as under-secretary of human rights of Corrientes in 2010.

Battle

British advance

The 3rd Battalion, The Parachute Regiment, made a desperate march across the hills north of Mount Simon to seize the key piece of high ground above the settlement of Estancia, nicknamed Estancia Farm. The weather conditions were atrocious, with the Paras marching through steep slippery hillocks to the objective. Nick Rose was a private in 6 Platoon under Lieutenant Jonathan Shaw.

The terrain dictated exactly how we advanced. A lot of the time if we were going along on tracks – what few tracks we did go on – we used Indian file, which is staggered file on either side of the track, like a zig zag. But there are great rivers of rock – big white boulders – and you have to cross them and then there's the heather and the gorse and its constantly wet. So the wind chill factor was – I think somebody said minus 40 degrees – and storm force winds and horizontal rain – a nightmare scenario. ... We are horrible, we're miserable as sin, all of us – we're missing home, want a dry fag, warm, dry boots, a cheese and onion sandwich and a bottle of blue top milk. I used to dream of these.

3 Para set up a patrol base near Murrell Bridge, two kilometres west of Mount Longdon on 3 June. From there they sent out their specialist patrols from D Company to scout out the Argentine positions on Mount Longdon. An example of a snatch patrol that failed to obtain a prisoner was provided by 3 PARA on the night of 4–5 June 1982. A three-man patrol from D Company consisting of Corporal Jerry Phillips and Privates Richard Absolon and Bill Hayward was sent out to the northern slopes of Mount Longdon. The small party was detailed to penetrate Sub-Lieutenant Juan Baldini's 1st Platoon on the western slopes to secure a prisoner, supported to their rear by a battery of six 105 mm field guns, under cover of which the specialist snipers shot at Baldini while another fired a 66 at one of the 1st Platoon mortar pits under Corporal Óscar Carrizo. The Argentine commanders reacted vigorously, and the sniper team found

themselves under prompt and accurate machinegun, artillery and mortar fire. There were no Argentine casualties. One British participant nevertheless claimed to have shot and killed two Argentines and demolished one mortar crew with a 66 mm anti-tank rocket at close range.

On the Argentine side, it was soon realised that the 7th Infantry Regiment Reconnaissance Platoon soldiers on the surrounding Wireless Ridge position were ill equipped to carry out their own patrolling. Thus, the Argentine Commando units, normally used for deep-recce had to take on this role. They were able to do so with some success and in the early hours of 7 June a combined patrol of the 601st Commando Company and 601st National Gendarmerie Special Forces Squadron was seen approaching Murrell Bridge. After several nights in the area Corporals Paul Haddon and Peter Brown and their patrols had just arrived at the bluff on the western bank of the Murrell River which Sergeant Ian Addle's patrol had been using as a base. Within a short space of time a sentry reported moving figures down near the bridge. The Paras opened up and a confused firefight developed in the darkness, with small arms, machinegun, LAW and Energa rifle grenades being exchanged. The Commando patrol under Captain Rubén Figueroa was very aggressive and before dawn had forced the Paras to withdraw, having to leave behind much of their equipment. Only one Argentine NCO was slightly wounded during the counter-ambush. From then on patrols had to be mounted closer to their own line. As the official history of the Parachute Regiment acknowledged:

'They were forced to evacuate their position rapidly, leaving behind their packs and radio, but succeeded in withdrawing without suffering any casualties. The location was checked on the evening of 8 June by another patrol, but there was no sign of the packs or radio, which meant the battalion's radio net could have been compromised.'

Nevertheless Colonel Pike and his company commanders on the eve of battle still held the Argentine commanders in low regard and did not expect them to put up much resistance. For this reason the British colonel hoped to surprise them by advancing as close to their forward platoon as possible under cover of darkness, before storming into their trenches with fixed bayonets. The three major objectives – Fly Half, Full Back and Wing Forward – were named after positions in Rugby. B Company would attack through Fly Half and proceed to Full Back, while A Company, followed by C Company if necessary, would do the same on Wireless Ridge.

But morale was still good in the 7th Regiment. Private Fabián Passaro of B Company served on Longdon with the 1st Platoon and remembers life at the time:

Most of us had adjusted to what we'd been landed in, we'd adjusted to the war. But *some* boys [identified in the book *Two Sides Of Hell/Los Dos Lados Del Infierno*] were still very depressed and, in many cases, were getting worse all the time. Of course, we were very fed up with wearing the same clothes for so many days, going without a shower, being so cold, eating badly. It was too many things together, quite apart from our natural fear of the war, the shelling and all that. But I think some of us were adapting better than others. There were kids who were very worried; and I tried to buoy them up a bit. 'Don't worry,' I told them. 'Nothing will happen, we're safe here. 'Don't you see they could never get right up here? There's one thousand of us; if they try to climb, we'll see them, we'll shoot the shit out of them.'"

When the 3 PARA's B Company (under Major Mike Argue) fixed bayonets to storm the Argentine 1st Platoon positions on Mount Longdon, they found themselves running into a minefield. The British sappers later counted some 1,500 anti-personnel mines sown along the western and northern slopes of Mount Longdon, 'but only two exploded' recalled Corporal Peter Cuxson, 'because the rest were frozen by ice'. 'Otherwise the final battle for Port Stanley would have been an altogether different story,' concludes the NCO who took an Argentine machine-gun position that night.

Assault on Longdon

As dusk set-in, 3 Para moved to their start-lines and, after a brief stop, began to make their four-hour long advance to their objectives. As B Company approached Mount Longdon Corporal Brian Milne stepped on a mine, which after a very silent approach, alerted Sub-Lieutenant Baldini's platoon of conscripts. More than 20 Argentinan soldiers emerged from their tents to lay down fire but most of the platoon was still struggling out of its sleeping bags when Lieutenant Ian Bickerdike's No. 4 Platoon was among them, machine-gunning and grenading the helpless Argentines. Corporal Stewart McLaughlin was in the thick of the action, clearing out an Argentine 7.62mm machinegun from the high ground overlooking the western slopes. He mustered his section, ordered them to fix bayonets and then led them up the hill into a hail of machinegun fire.

Lieutenant Jonathan Shaw's No. 6 Platoon, on the right flank of B Company, captured the summit of Fly Half with no fighting. However, they had missed half a dozen of Argentine conscripts of the forward platoon, having grenaded several abandoned bunkers, and they launched a fierce attack on the unsuspecting platoon, resulting in a number of casualties before the area was cleared. For three hours the hand-to-hand combat raged in the 1st Platoon sector, until the Paras drove out the defenders. All around the 1st Platoon position, small groups of soldiers were fighting for their lives. Privates Ben Gough and Dominic Gray managed to crawl undetected up to an Argentine bunker and crouched beside it as the Marine conscripts inside blasted away into the night. In unison the two Paras each pulled the pin out of a grenade and posted it through the firing slit of the bunker. The instant the grenade exploded the two jumped in the bunker and started to bayonet the two Marines. Private Gray killed a Marine by sticking his bayonet through his eye socket. Privates Gough and Grey were mentioned in despatches. Baldini himself appears to have been killed as he fired a machinegun. Corporal Dario Ríos was found lying dead with his platoon commander. Baldini's weapon and boots were removed for the use of the British soldiers. A photo of the dead lieutenant appeared in the original hardback edition of the book *Operation Corporate. The Story of the Falklands War*, 1982 (Viking Press, 1985) Also killed in the initial fighting was Cavalry Sergeant Jorge Alberto Ron and the Argentine forward artillery observation officer, Lieutenant Alberto Rolando Ramos, whose last message was that his position was surrounded. Sub-Lieutenant Baldini was awarded the Argentine Nation to the Valour in Combat Medal.

Just as it seemed as if the Paras would overwhelm 2nd Lieutenant Enrique Neirotti's 3rd Platoon on the southern half and Staff Sergeant Raúl González's 2nd Platoon on the northern half of the mountain, reinforcements from 2nd Lieutenant Hugo Quiroga's 1st Platoon, 10th Engineer Company on Full Back arrived to help Neirotti and González. Throughout the initial fighting in this sector, most of the Argentine positions on the saddle of the mountain held, the newly arrived engineers using head-mounted nightsights proving particularly deadly to the Paras.

Private Nick Rose in 6 Platoon resumes the story.

'Pete Grey stood up and went to throw a '42' grenade and he was shot by a sniper in his right forearm. We thought the grenade had gone off. We punched his arm down onto the ground to staunch the bleeding, believing he'd lost half his right forearm and hand, but it was still there and his arm bent at the forearm instead of the elbow – a horrible thing to watch. ...There's 'incoming' everywhere, loads of stuff going down the range and then 'bang' my pal 'Fester' [Tony Greenwood], gets it just above his left eye, only a yard away from me. That was a terrible thing. 'Fester' was such a lovely guy. Then it was 'Baz' Barratt. 'Baz' had gone back to try to get field dressings for Pete Grey and he was coming back 'bang' he got it in the back. This was when we just stalled as a platoon.' (Jon Cooksey, op. cit., p. 66)

The battle was going badly for Major Mike Argue. Argentine resistance was strong and well organized. At the centre of the mountain were Marine conscripts Jorge Maciel and Claudio Scaglione in a bunker with a heavy machinegun and Marine conscripts Luis Fernández and Sergio Giuseppetti with night-scope equipped rifles. Lieutenant Bickerdike and a signaller and Sergeant Ian McKay and a number of other men in No. 4 Platoon were attempting to perform reconnaissance on the Marine positions; in doing so, the platoon commander and signaller were wounded. Sergeant McKay realising something needed to be done, decided to attack the Marine heavy machinegun position that was causing so much trouble and so much misery. The assault was met by a hail of fire. Corporal Ian Bailey was seriously wounded, a Private killed and another wounded. Despite these losses Sergeant McKay, with complete disregard for his own safety for which he was to win posthumously the Victoria Cross, continued to charge the enemy position alone. Peter Harclerode who was granted open access to the war diary of the 3rd Battalion, and subsequently wrote *PARA!* (Arms & Armour Press, 1993), pointed out that McKay and his team cleared several Marine riflemen in position but failed to neutralize the heavy machinegun.

Corporal McLaughlin himself managed to crawl to within grenade-throwing range of the Marine heavy-machine-gun team, but despite several efforts with fragmentation grenades and 66 mm LAW rockets, he was unable to silence it.

Major Carrizo-Salvadores on Full Back had remained in touch with the Argentine commanders in Port Stanley: Around midnight I asked RHQ for infantry reinforcements, and I was given a rifle platoon from Captain Hugo García's C Company. First Lieutenant Raúl Fernando Castañeda gathered the sections of his platoon, hooked around First Sergeant Raúl González's 2nd Platoon that was already fighting and delivered a counterattack [at about 2 am local time]. The Platoon fought with great courage in fierce hand to hand combat and the battle raged for two more hours but gradually the enemy broke contact and withdrew while being engaged by artillery strikes'.

It was now the turn of the Argentines to attack. Major Carrizo-Salvadores manoeuvred Castañeda's reinforced platoon to close with 4 and 5 Platoons and meanwhile under the direction of an NCO, part of Castañeda's platoon converged on the British aid post. Colour Sergeant Brian Faulkner, seeing that more than 20 wounded Paras on the western slopes of the mountain were about to fall into the hands of one of the sections of Castañeda's platoon, deployed anyone fit enough to defend the British Regimental Aid Post. "I picked four blokes and got up on this high feature, and as I did so this troop [in fact a reinforced section of fifteen riflemen]of twenty, or thirty Argentines were coming towards us. We just opened fire on them. We don't know how many we killed, but they got what they deserved, because none of them were left standing when we'd finished with them." said Faulkner

Things were so bad that Major Mike Argue's company ceased firing and devoted their full efforts to withdrawing from Fly Half. Peter Harclerode, a noted British historian of the Parachute Regiment, went on record, saying that:

'under covering fire, Nos. 4 and 5 Platoons withdrew, but another man was killed and others wounded in the process. At that point, Lieutenant Colonel Hew Pike and his 'R' Group arrived on the scene and Major Argue briefed him on the situation. Shortly afterwards, Company Sergeant Major Weekes reported that both platoons had pulled back to a safe distance and that all the wounded had been recovered. The dead, however, had to be left where they had fallen. Meanwhile, on the southern slope of the objective, the wounded from No. 6 Platoon were being evacuated while the rest remained under cover of the rocks.

The British 3rd Commando Brigade

commander, Brigadier Julian Thompson was reported as having said: "I was on the point of withdrawing my Paras from Mount Longdon. We couldn't believe that these teenagers disguised as soldiers were causing us to suffer many casualties."

By the time the 21 survivors of Castañeda's 46-man platoon had worked their way off the mountain, they were utterly exhausted. One of them, Private Leonardo Rondi, was sporting a maroon beret – taken from a dead parachute soldier. Private Rondi, having dodged groups of Paras to deliver messages to Castañeda's section leaders, had found a Para behind a rock (it may have been Sergeant McKay) and took his red beret and SLR which he later gave to the Argentine commanders as trophies. Rondi was awarded the Argentine Nation to the Valour in Combat Medal.

Following the unexpectedly fierce fighting on Fly Half, Major Argue pulled back Nos. 4, and 5 Platoons, and 29 Commando Regiment began pounding the mountain from Mount Kent, after which a left flanking attack was put in. Under heavy fire, the remnants of 4 and 5 Platoons under Lieutenant Mark Cox advanced upon their objective of Full Back, taking some casualties from Casteñeda's platoon as they did so. As he was clearing the Argentine position, Private Grey was injured from a headshot but refused to be evacuated until Major Argue had consolidated his troops properly in their positions on Fly Half. Private Kevin Connery personally dispatched three wounded Argentines in this action. The Paras could not move any further without taking unacceptable losses and so were pulled back to the western end of Mount Longdon, with the orders for Major David Collett's A Company to move through B Company and assault, from the west, the eastern objective of Full Back, a heavily defended position, with covering fire being given from Support Company.

Second Lieutenants John Kearton and Ian Moore mustered their platoons near the western summit and had briefed them on how to deal with the enemy. They soon attacked the position in bitter close-combat, clearing the position of the Argentine defenders with rifle, grenade and bayonet. As A Company was clearing the final positions, Corporal McLaughlin was injured by a Czekalski recoilless rifle round fired from Wireless Ridge. Unfortunately the brave NCO was killed by a mortar bomb fired from RI 7's C Company on Wireless Ridge as he made his way to the aid post. The Argentines rigorously defended Full Back. Although already wounded, Corporal Manuel Medina of Castañeda's platoon took over a recoilless rifle detachment and personally fired along the ridge at Support Company killing three Paras, including Private Peter Heddicker, who took the full force of the 105 mm round, and wounding three others. Major Carrizo-Salvadores abandoned his command bunker on Full Back only when a MILAN missile smashed into some rocks just behind him. In the command bunker Major Collett found 2,000 cigarettes which he gave to the smokers in his company.

Aftermath

The battle and the immediate Argentine covering fire that followed lasted twelve-hours and had been costly to both sides. 3 PARA lost seventeen killed during the battle, one Royal Engineer attached to 3 PARA was also killed. Two of the 3 PARA dead – Privates Ian Scrivens and Jason Burt – were only seventeen years old, and Private Neil Grose was killed on his 18th birthday. A total of forty British paratroopers were wounded during the battle. A further four Paras and one REME were killed and seven Paratroopers were wounded in the two-day shelling that followed that was directed from Sub-Lieutenant Marcelo de Marco of the 5th Marines on Tumbledown Mountain. The Argentines suffered 31 dead and 120 wounded, with fifty also being taken prisoner.

Lance-Corporal Vincent Bramley was patrolling the western half of Mount Longdon when he was confronted with the full horror of the night combat. The 3 PARA NCO and keen writer stumbled upon the bodies of five Paratroopers killed by the forward Argentine platoon.

'A few bullets whizzed overhead and smashed into the rocks. A corporal shouted that Tumbledown was firing at us. We ran into a tight gap in the path of all came to an abrupt halt, as it was a dead end. Four or five bodies lay sprawled there, close together. This time they were our own men: the camouflaged Para smocks hit my eyes immediately. CSM [Company-Sergeant-Major] Weekes was standing over them like a guardian, screaming at some of his men to cover the further end of the path and a small crest. The CSM and Sergeant P [Pettinger] exchanged quick words. I wasn't listening; my mind was totally occupied with looking into the crags for the enemy. I turned and looked at our own lads, dead on the ground, mowed down when they tried to rush through this gap. I felt both anger and sadness. The CSM's face showed the strain of having seen most of his company either wounded or shot dead. That night's fighting was written in every line of his face.'

The battle was particularly brutal with little quarter being shown by either side.

Decorations

The 3rd Battalion of the Parachute Regiment won numerous decorations for this action:

- One Victoria Cross (Sergeant Ian McKay)
- One Distinguished Service Order (Lieutenant-Colonel Hew Pike)
- Two Military Crosses (Majors Mike Argue and David Collett)
- Two Distinguished Conduct Medals (Colour Sergeant Brian Faulkner and Sergeant John Pettinger)
- Three Military Medals (Sergeant Des Fuller, Corporal Ian Bailey, and Private Richard Absolon)
- Numerous Mentioned in Despatches

Source (edited): "http://en.wikipedia.org/wiki/Battle_of_Mount_Longdon"

Battle of Mount Tumbledown

The **Battle of Mount Tumbledown** was an engagement in the Falklands War, one of a series of battles that took place during the British advance towards Stanley.

Overview

On the night of 13 June – 14 June 1982, the British launched an assault on Mount Tumbledown, one of the highest points near the town of Stanley, and succeeded in driving Argentinian forces from the mountain. This close-quarters night battle was later dramatised in the BBC film *Tumbledown*.

The attacking British forces consisted of the 2nd Battalion, Scots Guards, mortar detachments from 42 Commando, Royal Marines and the 1/7th Duke of Edinburgh's Own Gurkha Rifles, as well as support from a troop of the Blues and Royals equipped with two Scorpion and two Scimitar armored vehicles. The Argentinian forces defending the mountains were Commander Carlos Robacio's 5th Marine Infantry Battalion (BIM 5).

Prior to the British landings, the Argentinian marine battalion had been brought up to brigade strength by a company of the Amphibious Engineers Company (CKIA), a battery of the 1st Marine Artillery Battalion (BIAC), and three Tigercat SAM batteries of the 1st Marine Anti-Aircraft Regiment, as well as a heavy machine-gun company of the Headquarters Battalion (BICO). As part of the British plan, the 1st Battalion the 7th Gurkha Rifles (1/7 GR) was given the task of capturing the sub-hill of Mount William held by O Company, the 5th Marine Battalion's reserve, and then allowing the Welsh Guards through to seize Sapper Hill, the final obstacle before the town of Stanley. The attack was supported by naval gunfire from HMS *Active*'s 4.5 inch gun.

At the time of the battle, N Company held Mount Tumbledown. Mount William was just south of Tumbledown and the Marine battalion's O Company was on its lower slopes. B Company 6th Regiment was in reserve behind N Company. M Company occupied Sapper Hill. The Argentinian defenders held firm under the British 'softening up' bombardment, which began at 7:30 local time. As Major Oscar Jaimet recalled in *Razor's Edge*, *I heard the cries of the wounded calling for their comrades, twelve men wounded before nightfall. We thought we had suffered before, but what luxury and comfort compared to this.*

During the battle, the 5th Marines Command Post took five direct hits, but Commander Robacio emerged unscathed.

Early moves

On the morning of 13 June, the Scots Guards were moved by helicopter from their position at Bluff Cove to an assembly area near Goat Ridge, west of Mount Tumbledown. The British plan called for a diversionary attack south of Mount Tumbledown by a small number of Scots Guards assisted by the four light tanks of the Blues and Royals, whilst the main attack came as a three-phase silent advance from the west of Mount Tumbledown. In the first phase, G company would take the western end of the mountain; in the second phase, Left Flank would pass through the area taken by G company to capture the center of the summit; and in the third phase, Right Flank would pass through Left Flank to secure the eastern end of Tumbledown. A daytime assault was initially planned, but was postponed at the British battalion commander's request. In a meeting with his company commanders the consensus was that the long uphill assault across the harsh ground of Tumbledown would be suicidal.

Diversion

At 8:30 p.m. on 13 June the diversionary attack began. The 2nd Bn Scots Guards' Reconnaissance Platoon, commanded by Major Richard Bethell (a former SAS officer), and supported by four light tanks of the Blues and Royals, attacked the Argentinian marine company entrenched on the lower slopes of Mount William. On Mount William's southern slopes, one of the tanks was taken out of action by a booby trap. The initial advance was unopposed, but a heavy firefight broke out when British troops made contact with Argentine defences. The Argentines opened fire, killing two British soldiers and wounding four. After two hours of hard fighting, the British secured the position.

Fearing a counter-attack, the British platoon withdrew into an undetected minefield, and were forced to abandon their dead. Two men were wounded covering the withdrawal and four more were wounded by mines. The explosions prompted the Argentine marine commanders to order the 81 mm mortar platoon on Mount William to open fire on the minefield and the likely withdrawal route of anyone attacking Mount William. The barrage lasted for about forty minutes and more British casualties would have been suffered if the mortar bombs had not landed on soft peat, which absorbed most of the blasts.

Night attack

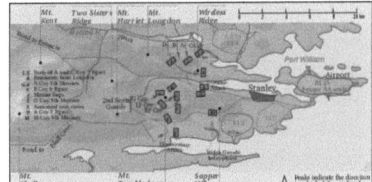

Final Actions, 13 to 14 June 1982

At 9 p.m., half an hour after the start of the diversionary attack, Major Iain Dalzel-Job's G Company started its advance of nearly two miles. Reaching its objective undetected, the company found the western end of the mountain undefended and occupied it easily. Major John Kiszely's Left Flank passed through them and reached the central region of the peak unopposed, but then came under heavy fire. The Argentinians, later learned to be of company strength, directed mortar, grenade, machine gun, and small arms fire from very close range at the British company, killing two British soldiers: Guardsman Ronald Tanbini and Sergeant John Simeon. Marine Sub-Lieutenant Héctor Mino's 5th Platoon, Amphibious Engineer Company, held the rocks to the right of Marine Sub-Lieutenant Carlos Vázquez's 4th Platoon, 5th Marines. In the center and to the left of the 4th Platoon were Second Lieutenant Óscar Silva's RI 4 platoon, which had recently fought well on Goat Ridge. For four or five hours, three platoons of Argentinian riflemen, machine gunners, and mortar men pinned the British down. To help identify the bunkers, the Guardsmen fired flares into the summit. The Guardsmen traded 66 mm rockets and 84 mm anti-tank rounds with the Argentinians, protected in their rock bunkers. The enemy refused to budge and the Scots Guards could hear some of the Argentinians shouting obscene phrases in English and even singing as they fought. Meanwhile, two Royal Navy frigates, HMS *Yarmouth* and HMS *Active*, were pounding Tumbledown with 4.5 inch guns. At one stage Colonel Scott thought the 2nd Battalion Scots Guards might have to withdraw and attack again the next night, 'The old nails were being bitten a bit, if we had been held on Tumbledown it might have encouraged them to keep on fighting.'

The fighting was hard going for Left Flank. The Argentinians had well dug-in machine guns and snipers. At 2:30 a.m., however, a second British assault overwhelmed the Argentinian defences. British troops swarmed the mountaintop and drove the Argentinians out, at times fighting with fixed bayonets. Major Kiszely, who was to become a senior general after the war, was the first man into the enemy position, personally shooting two enemy conscripts and bayoneting a third, his bayonet breaking in two. Seeing their company commander among the Argentinians inspired 14 and 15 Platoons to make the final dash across open ground to get within bayoneting distance of the marines. Kiszely and six other Guardsmen suddenly found themselves standing on top of the mountain, looking down on Stanley under street lighting and with vehicles moving along the roads. The Argentinians now counter-attacked and a burst of machine gun fire from 3rd Platoon of Second Lieutenant Augusto La Madrid injured three British men, including Lieutenant Alasdair Mitchell, commander of 15 Platoon. A bullet passed through the compass secured on Kiszely's belt. For his bayonet charge Major Kiszely was awarded the Military Cross.

Morning

By 6 a.m., Left Flank's attack had clearly stalled and had cost the British company 7 men killed and 18 wounded. On the eastern half of the mountain the platoon of conscripts of La Madrid were still holding out, so Colonel Scott ordered Right Flank to push on to clear the final positions. Major Simon Price sent 2 and 3 Platoons forward, preceded by a barrage of 66 mm rockets to clear the forward RI 6 platoon. Major Price placed 1 Platoon high up in the rocks to provide fire support for the assault troops. Lieutenant Robert Lawrence led 3 Platoon around to the right of the Argentinian platoon, hoping to take the Argentinians by surprise. They were detected, however, and the British were briefly pinned down by gunfire before a bayonet charge overwhelmed the Argentinian defenders. Lance-Corporal Graham Rennie of 3 Platoon in the book *5th Infantry Brigade in the Falklands* (Pen & Sword Books, 2003) later described the attack:

Our assault was initiated by a Guardsman killing a sniper, which was followed by a volley of 66 mm anti-tanks rounds. We ran forward in extended line, machine-gunners and riflemen firing from the hip to keep the enemy heads down, enabling us to cover the open ground in the shortest possible time. Halfway across the open ground 2 Platoon went to ground to give covering fire support, enabling us to gain a foothold on the enemy position. From then on we fought from crag to crag, rock to rock, taking out pockets of enemy and lone riflemen, all of who resisted fiercely.

As La Madrid withdrew in the face of a superior assaulting force, the platoons under Second Lieutenant Aldo Franco and Guillermo Robredo moved in from the eastern edge of the mountain to try to help La Madrid and the Marine 2nd platoon (under Second Lieutenant Marcelo Oruezabala) holding the saddle between Mounts Tumbledown and William. Advancing out of the central region of Tumbledown Mountain, the British again came under heavy fire from the Argentinians, but by advancing in pairs under covering fire, the British succeeded in clearing those RI 6 Company platoons as well, gaining firm control of the mountain's eastern side. Right Flank had achieved this at the cost of five wounded, including Lt. Lawrence. In his moment of victory on the eastern slopes, Lawrence was almost killed when a bullet fired by an Argentine sniper tore off the side of his head. He was awarded the Military Cross for bravery, but he spent a year in a wheelchair and was almost totally paralyzed. The Argentinian sniper with a FAL rifle had helped cover the Argentinean retreat, firing shots at a Scout helicopter evacuating wounded off Tumbledown and injuring two Guardsmen before the Scots Guards mortally wounded him in a hail of gunfire.

Aftermath

By 9:00 a.m., the Scots Guards had gained the high ground east of Tumbledown Mountain and the Gurkhas commenced deploying across the heavily shelled saddle from Tumbledown south to Mount William, which they took with a loss of eight wounded. The 2nd Battalion Scots Guards had lost 8 dead and 43 wounded, the Welsh Guards had lost 1 dead, the Royal Engineers had lost 1 dead, and the Gurkhas had lost 10 wounded. One Guardsmen lost his way in the dark. The Guardsman hid for more than a month, not realizing that the fighting was over. The Guards took 30 prisoners, several of them RI 6 soldiers. The bodies of 30 Argentine Army and Marine soldiers were strewn over the 5th Marine Battalion perimeter.

Unwilling to abandon the hill, Commander Carlos Robacio on Sapper Hill counter-attacked and drove back the Guardsmen. Only the personal intervention of Colonel Félix Aguiar, the 10th Brigade Chief of Staff, brought the fighting to an end. The 5th Marines worked their way back into Stanley, leaving M Company to cover the retreat. At the foot of the hill there was an enormous minefield. A group of Sappers went ahead to clear a path across the mines, but when the Welsh Guardsmen advanced they found Sapper Hill abandoned. The delay caused by the mines may have saved lives. The Marine companies had been deeply entrenched and were well equipped with heavy machine guns. To Guardsman Tracy Evens, the Sapper Hill positions looked impregnable:

We were led to an area that the company would rest at for the night, I still took in the fact the Argies had prepared Sapper Hill well, they had depth positions that would have made the task of taking it very hard. (Taken from the diary of Guardsman Tracy Evens)

During the battle, soldier Philip Williams was knocked unconscious by an explosion, and left for dead. When he came to, the rest of the British soldiers had gone. Williams' parents were informed of his "death" and a memorial service held for him. After seven weeks he found his way back to civilization, to find himself accused of desertion by the media and fellow soldiers.

For the courage displayed in the attack, men from the 2nd Scots Guards were awarded one Distinguished Service Order, two Military Crosses, two Distinguished Conduct Medals (one posthumously), and two Military Medals. Men from 9 Para Squadron, Royal Engineers, were awarded two Military Medals and Captain Sam Drennan, the Army Air Corps Scout pilot who had picked up the injured soldiers under fire and a former Scots Guards NCO, received the Distinguished Flying Cross.

Carlos Robacio, BIM5 commander, was awarded the Argentine Nation to the Valour in Combat Medal and the battalion itself was condecorated by the Argentine Congress in 2002

Due to his actions in both Two Sisters and Tumbledown, SC 62 Oscar Ismael Poltronieri of LaMadrid's RIM-6 section was awarded the Argentine Nation to the Heroic Valour in Combat Cross, Argentina's highest military decoration. He's the only conscript soldier in his nation's history who has received this honor.

Source (edited): "http://en.wikipedia.org/wiki/Battle_of_Mount_Tumbledown"

Battle of San Carlos (1982)

The **Battle of San Carlos** was a major battle between aircraft and ships that lasted from 21 to 25 May 1982 during the British landings on the shores of San Carlos Water (which became known as "Bomb Alley") in the 1982 Falklands War (Spanish: *Guerra de las Malvinas*). Low-flying land-based Argentine jet aircraft made repeated attacks on ships of the British Task Force. It was the first time in history that a modern surface fleet armed with surface-to-air missiles and with air cover backed up by STOVL carrier-based aircraft defended against full-scale air strikes. The British sustained severe losses and damage, but were able to create and consolidate a beachhead and land troops.

Background

After the Argentine invasion of the Falkland Islands the United Kingdom initiated Operation Corporate sending a Task Force 12000 km south in order to retake the islands. Under the codename Operation Sutton the British forces planned amphibious landings around San Carlos, on an inlet located off Falkland Sound, the strait between East Falkland and West Falkland. The location was chosen as the landing force would be protected by the terrain against Exocet and submarine attacks, and it was distant enough from Stanley to prevent a rapid reaction from Argentine land troops stationed there. The landing took the Argentines completely by surprise; Argentine Navy officers had considered that the location was not a good choice for such an operation, and had left the zone without major defences.

Argentine aircraft

Argentine forces operated under range and payload limitations as they had limited refueling resources and were operating at maximum range.

- A-4 Skyhawk: The A-4 was used by both the Argentine Air Force (FAA) and Argentine Naval Aviation (COAN). In spite of using two 295-gallons drop tanks, they needed aerial refuelling twice during missions. Bomb load used during the conflict was one British-made 1000 lb (Mk 17) unguided bomb or four 227 kg Spanish/American built retarding tail bombs. The aircraft were armed with two 20mm Colt Mk 12 cannon
- IAI Dagger: The Israeli-built Mirage 5 did not have aerial refuelling capacity, and even using two 550-gallon drop tanks to carry extra fuel, they were flying at the absolute limit of their range. Their main weapon during the conflict was the British-made 1000 lb (Mk 17) unguided bomb. They retained their 30 mm DEFA cannon
- Mirage IIIEA: The French-built interceptor has an internal fuel tank smaller than that of the Dagger, so they could not fly low enough to escort the strike aircraft. They carried a pair of R550 Magic IR missiles in their high-altitude flights to the islands, but the British Harrier combat air patrols concentrated on the low-flying bombers.
- FMA IA-58 Pucara: The Argentine-built counter-insurgency aircraft operated from the Goose Green grass airstrip during the battle. The aircraft were armed with rocket pods, two 20 mm cannons and four

7.62 mm machine guns.

British amphibious force

British air cover was provided for the first time by "Harrier carriers". These small carriers deployed only short-take-off, vertical-landing Harriers, subsonic aircraft with less range and payload than land or conventional carrier-based aircraft.

800 NAS Sea Harrier FRS1 from HMS *Hermes*

- Air Cover:
  - Aircraft carrier HMS *Hermes* (R12)
    - 800 Squadron (BAE Sea Harrier)
    - 809 Squadron (BAE Sea Harrier)
  - Aircraft carrier HMS *Invincible* (R05)
    - 801 Squadron (BAE Sea Harrier)
    - 809 Squadron (BAE Sea Harrier)
- Landing force: HMS *Fearless*, HMS *Intrepid*, RFA *Sir Geraint*, RFA *Sir Tristram*, RFA *Sir Galahad*, RFA *Sir Percivale*, RFA *Sir Lancelot*, SS *Canberra*, RFA *Fort Austin*, *Europic Ferry 4* and *Elk 5*.
- Escort force: HMS *Antrim*, HMS *Coventry*, HMS *Broadsword*, HMS *Brilliant*, HMS *Ardent*, HMS *Antelope*, HMS *Argonaut*, HMS *Plymouth* and HMS *Yarmouth*

Engagements

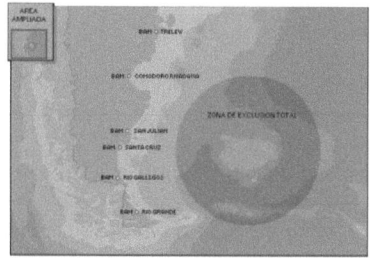

Argentine airbases: Distances to Port Stanley Airport: Trelew: 580 nautical miles (1,070 km), Comodoro Rivadavia: 480 nautical miles (890 km), San Julián: 425 nautical miles (787 km), Rio Gallegos: 435 nautical miles (806 km) and Rio Grande: 380 nautical miles (700 km). Due to the distance required to fly to the islands, two minutes was the average time Argentine attack aircraft had available in the target area.

This is a list of the main sorties carried out by Argentine air units showing approximate local time, Aircraft and Call signal.

May 21

The Argentine Army force on site was a section from the 25th Infantry Regiment named *Combat team Güemes* (Spanish: *Equipo de Combate Güemes*) located at Fanning Head. The British fleet entered San Carlos during the night and at 02:50 was spotted by *EC Güemes* which opened fire with 81mm mortars and two recoilless 105mm rifles. They were soon engaged by British naval gunfire and a 25-man SBS team and forced to retreat, losing their communications equipment but shooting down two Gazelle helicopters with small-arms fire.

1st Lt Carlos Daniel Esteban from *EC Güemes* informed Goose Green garrison about the landings at 08:22 (he was finally evacuated by helicopter on May 26). The Argentine high command at Stanley initially suggested that a landing operation was not feasible at San Carlos and the operation was just a diversion. Finally, at 10:00, a COAN Aermacchi MB-339 jet based on the islands was dispatched to San Carlos on a reconnaissance flight. In the meantime, the FAA had already started launching their mainland-based aircraft at 09:00.

Naval Aviation Aermacchi MB-339

- 10:15 : COAN MB339 4-A-115. Lt Guillermo Owen Crippa in a reconnaissance flight flew over the landing force twice to determine the exact composition of the fleet, earning the highest national military decoration, the Argentine Nation to the Heroic Valour in Combat Cross. He attacked HMS *Argonaut* and an unidentified RFA ship with guns and rockets, then withdrew. Painting of Lt Crippas solo attack on the frigate "Argonaut"
- 10:15 : FAA Pucara *Tigre*. Three (of four) planes scrambled from Goose Green and were engaged by gunfire from HMS *Ardent*. Cpt Benítez was shot down by a Stinger missile fired by the Special Air Service; he ejected and walked back to his base, arriving at 19:00. The other two pilots, Mj Tomba and 1st Lt Micheloud, fired 2.75 inch rockets at a shed apparently used by British forces as an observation post, but were intercepted by two Sea Harriers during their escape. Mj Tomba was shot down (ejecting safely) by pilot Nigel Ward, while Lt Micheloud escaped and landed at Port Stanley's airfield.
- 10:20 : FAA MIIIEA. Four aircraft made a diversion north of the islands.
- 10:25 : FAA Dagger *Leon*. From San Julian, Cpt Dimeglio and Lt Castillo attacked HMS *Antrim* with their 30mm cannon. Their 1,000 lb (450 kg) bombs failed to explode.

- 10:30 : FAA Dagger *Ñandu*. From Rio Grande, Tierra del Fuego, Cpt Rodhe and Lt Bean attacked HMS *Argonaut*, Lt Bean was shot down by a Sea Wolf SAM from HMS *Broadsword*; *Broadsword* was attacked by pilot Cpt Janet.

HMS *Fearless* at San Carlos

- 10:35 : FAA Dagger *Zorro*. Cpt Dellepine, Cpt Diaz and Cpt Aguirre-Faget bombed and strafed HMS *Brilliant* but the bombs hang-up.
- 10:50 : FAA Dagger *Perro*. Mj Martinez, Cpt Moreno and Lt Volponi attacked HMS *Antrim*. Their 1,000 lb (450 kg) bombs did not explode, but one of them hit the stern of the destroyer, which also received damage from 30 mm strafing. During their escape, Sea Harriers launched Sidewinders against the Daggers but they fell short.
- 12:45 : FAA A-4C *Pato*. Cpt Almoño, Cpt Garcia, 1st Lt Daniel Manzotti and Lt Nestor Lopez were intercepted by Sea Harriers; Manzotti and López were shot down and killed by Sidewinders.
- 12:45 : FAA A-4B *Mula*. Cpt Carballo and Ensign Carmona. *Mula 2* attacked an unknown ship, most probably the abandoned Argentine cargo vessel *Rio Carcaraña*, and withdrew, Carballo continued alone and attacked HMS *Ardent* straddling her with two bombs, both of which failed to explode.
- 13:37 : FAA A-4B *Leo*. 1st Lt Filippini, Lt Autiero, Lt Osses, Lt Robledo and Ensign Vottero hit HMS *Argonaut* with 1,000 lb (450 kg) bombs which did not explode, with one crashing through her Sea Cat magazine, detonating two missiles and causing damage.
- 14:30 : FAA MIIIEA. Two aircraft took off as a diversion.
- 14:35 : FAA Dagger *Cueca* Cpt Mir Gonzales, Cpt Robles, 1st Lt Luna and Lt Bernhard were intercepted by Sea Harriers, and Lt Luna was hit by a Sidewinder but ejected safely. The other three pilots attacked HMS *Ardent* and return to base.

Gate guardian painted in the colours of *3-A-314*, the last A-4Q to attack HMS *Ardent*

- 14:53 : FAA Dagger *Laucha* Mj Puga, 1st Lt Román attack HMS *Brilliant*. The third pilot attacked an unknown ship, probably HMS *Antrim*.
- 14:58 : FAA Dagger *Raton* Mj Piuma, Cpt Donadille and 1st lt Senn were intercepted by Sea Harriers of Nigel Ward and Lt Thomas. The Daggers dropped their ordnance -2 fuel tanks and one 1,000 lb (450 kg)- and tried to escape, but the three were shot down by Sidewinders, with all pilots ejecting safely. After recovering the pilots, the FAA realized that the San Julian-based Daggers' approach corridor had been discovered and made efforts to correct the situation.
- 15:15 : COAN A-4Q *Tabanos*. Cpt Philipi, Lt Arca and Lt Marquez hit HMS *Ardent* with several 500 lb (230 kg) retarding tail bombs and cannon fire. Two aircraft were shot down by Sea Harriers during their escape, killing Lt Marcelo Márquez. Lt. Philippi ejected safely and, after being sheltered by local farmer Tony Blake during the night, he rejoined the Argentine forces. The third A-4Q, Lt Arca, was damaged and the pilot baled out into the sea approximately 800 to 1,000 meters off Cape Pembroke, Port Stanley. Arca was rescued from the water by Capt. Jorge "Picho" Svendsen's Huey UH-1H from the Army's 601 Helicopter Battalion. Both crew were decorated with the Valour in Combat Medal.
- 17:02 : FAA A-4C : No ships found.
- 17:12 : FAA A-4B : No ships found.

May 22

Bad weather over the Patagonia airfields prevented the Argentines from carrying out most of their air missions; only a few Skyhawks managed to reach the islands. The British completed their surface-to-air Rapier battery launcher deployments.

May 23

HMS *Antelope*

- 13:30 : FAA A-4B *Nene*. Four A-4Bs (Carballo, 1st Lt Guadagnini, Lt Rinke and Ensign Gomez) attacked HMS *Broadsword* and HMS *Antelope*. Carballo's plane was damaged by a Sea Cat missile, fired from *Antelope*, during his bombing run, so he broke off the attack and returned to Rio Gallegos. A second Argentine plane dropped a 1,000 lb (450 kg) bomb on *Antelope*s starboard side, killing Crewman Mark R. Stephens. Lieutenant Guadagnini was hit and killed by HMS Antelope's 20mm cannon and crashed through her main mast while carrying out his bombing run; his bombs pierced the frigate's hull without exploding. After the attack,

one of these detonated while being defused, sinking the ship.
- 13:45 : COAN A-4Q *Tabanos*. Cpt Castro Fox, Cpt Zubizarreta and Lt Benitez attacked HMS *Broadsword*, HMS *Yarmouth* and HMS *Antelope* without visible success. Cpt Carlos María Zubizarreta was killed in Rio Grande, Tierra del Fuego when his parachute did not fully open after he ejected from his A-4Q due to a tyre bursting on landing with his bombs still loaded. The plane stopped by itself and did not suffer any damage.
- 15:10 : FAA Dagger *Puñal*. Mj Martinez and Lt Volponi intercepted by Sea Harriers, which shot down the second aircraft, whilst Martinez returned to base.
- 15:10 : FAA Dagger *Daga*. Struck targets inside Ajax Bay
- 15:10 : FAA Dagger *Coral*. Struck targets inside Ajax Bay

May 24

IAI Dagger

- 10:15 FAA A-4B *Chispa*. Four A-4Bs (Com Mariel, 1st Lt Sanchez, Lt Roca, Lt Cervera and Ensign Moroni) attacked ships inside the bay. RFA *Sir Lancelot* was hit by a 1,000 lb (450 kg) bomb, which did not explode. Two LCUs are also attacked.
- 11:02 FAA Dagger *Azul*. Cpt Mir Gonzalez, Cpt Maffeis, Cpt Robles and Lt Bernhardt attacked unidentified ships, probably RFA *Sir Bedivere*, inside the bay.
- 11:07 FAA Dagger *Plata*. Cpt Dellepiane, 1st Lt Musso and Lt Callejo stroke ground targets with 500 lb (230 kg) retarding tail bombs.
- 11:08 FAA Dagger *Oro*. Mj Puga, Cpt Diaz and 1st Lt Castillo were intercepted and shot down by Sea Harriers. Castillo was killed and the other two ejected safely.
- 11:20 FAA A-4C *Halcon*. Cpt Pierini, 1st Lt Ureta and Lt Mendez were intercepted by Sea Harriers but managed to return to base.
- 11:30 FAA A-4C *Jaguar*. 1st Lt Vazquez, Lt Bono and Ensign Martinez attacked unidentified ships, possibly RFA *Sir Galahad*, inside the bay. The three aircraft all received battle damage with Bono's aircraft crashing during the return flight. The other two Skyhawks were rescued by a KC-130 tanker, which approached the islands and delivered 30,000 litres of fuel while accompanying them to the airfield at San Julian.

On May 24 night there was a kind of mutiny between the Argentine pilots on the continent, who said they would refuse to continue flying if the Army and Navy did not join the battle. General Galtieri, acting president of Argentina, decided to visit Comodoro Rivadavia the next day, May 25 (Argentina's National Day), to try to convince them to keep fighting, but when he arrived in the morning the pilots had changed their minds and were already flying to the islands.

May 25

Skyhawk departing to the islands

- 09:00 FAA A-4B *Marte*. Cpt Hugo Palaver's aircraft was damaged in a friendly fire incident when he and Lt Daniel Gálvez accidentally flew over Goose Green and strafed the pier there, in the belief that they were over Ajax Bay. The main anti-aircraft artillery identified the fighters as friendly and did not fire, but soldiers on the ground engaged with small arms fire. When they returned to the strait, Palaver was shot down by a Sea Dart missile fired by HMS Coventry
- 12:25 FAA A-4C *Toro*. Cpt Garcia, Lt Lucero (C-319), Lt Paredi and Ensign Issac attacked ships inside the bay, probably RFA *Sir Lancelot*; after the attack Lucero was shot down by a Sea Cat missile fired from HMS Yarmouth. He successfully ejected over the landing force, was rescued and then transferred to the hospital ship SS *Uganda*. Another Sea Dart, fired by HMS Coventry, shot down Garcia, whose aircraft had been damaged by small arms fire during the attack, to the North of San Carlos. Cpt Garcia ejected, but was not recovered and died. Ensign Isaac was losing fuel but was rescued by the KC-130, which accompanied him to his base while refuelling him in flight.
- 15:20 FAA A-4B *Vulcano*. Cpt Carballo and Lt Carlos Rinke attacked HMS *Broadsword*, damaging the frigate's communication systems and hydraulics and electrics and shattering the nose of her Sea Lynx helicopter
- 15:20 FAA A-4B *Zeus*. 1st Lt Velazco and Ensign Barrionuevo sank destroyer HMS *Coventry* after hitting the ship with three 500 lb (230 kg) bombs.

Aftermath

British troops Yomp to Stanley

" I think the Argentine pilots are showing great bravery, it would be foolish of me to say anything else "

—*John Nott British Defence Minister*

In spite of the massive air defence network, the Argentine pilots were able to attack their targets but, although undoubtedly brave, some serious procedural failures prevented them from getting better results - most notably problems with their bombs' fuses. Thirteen bombs hit British ships without detonating. Lord Craig, the retired Marshal of the Royal Air Force, is said to have remarked: "Six better fuses and we would have lost". The British warships, although themselves suffering most of the attacks, were successful in keeping the strike aircraft away from the landing ships, which were well inside the bay.

With the British troops on Falklands soil, a land campaign followed until Argentine General Mario Menéndez surrendered to British Major General Jeremy Moore on June 14 in Stanley.

The subsonic Harrier jump-jet, armed with the most advanced variant of the Sidewinder air-to-air missile, proved capable as an air superiority fighter.

The actions had a profound impact on later naval practice. During the 1980s most warships from navies around the world were retrofitted with close-in weapon systems and guns for self-defence. First reports of the number of Argentine aircraft shot down by British missile systems were subsequently revised down.

Source (edited): "http://en.wikipedia.org/wiki/Battle_of_San_Carlos_(1982)"

Battle of Seal Cove

The **Battle of Seal Cove** was a minor naval action west of Lively Island, during the 1982 Falklands War. On May 22, 1982, while supporting Operation Sutton off San Carlos Bay, the British frigates HMS *Brilliant* and HMS *Yarmouth* received orders to stop and seize the Argentine armed coastal supply boat ARA *Monsunen*. The coaster *Monsunen* was actually a small British vessel that had been captured in the course of the Argentine invasion. The ship was spotted by a RAF Harrier while sailing from Fox Bay towards Stanley with a cargo of 150 fuel drums and 250 flour sacks.

The engagement

On the very first hours of May 23, a Sea Lynx identified the *Monsunen* while the latter was heading to the north, west of Lively Island. After a surrender order was radioed to the motorboat, another helicopter transporting a SBS team tried to intercept her. The aircraft was greeted with heavy machine gun and small arms fire, so it was forced to abort the mission. At the same time, the coastal ship's radar detected the British squadron about eight miles to stern and approaching aggressively.

Almost immediately, HMS *Yarmouth* began to fire her 4.5 inch (114 mm) deck gun on the Argentine vessel, forcing her to manoeuvre in order to avoid the incoming rounds. When the distance fell to 4 miles, Captain Gopcevich, the Argentine commander, decided that the only way to deceive the British radar was to beach the boat on Seal Cove, a large inlet nearby.

Shortly after he succeeded in running aground his ship and ordering the crew to abandon her, the British shelling resumed. The fire was inaccurate and aimed at the general area of landing. In the process of evacuating the vessel, one of the ratings fell overboard and suffered some serious bruises, but he was successfully rescued by a young sailor. The crew members took refuge in an improvised inland shelter.

Aftermath

After effectively losing the track of their small enemy, the British frigates gave up and returned to San Carlos waters. *Monsunen* was found by her complement at dawn, with her engine still running, apparently after refloating by the rising tide. However, a sling had become entangled with her propeller, disabling the transmission.

HMS *Yarmouth*

With the ship's speed now dramatically reduced, Gopcevich radioed for help to Stanley.

A few hours later, another British trawler seized by the Argentines, ARA *Forrest*, towed the *Monsunen* to Darwin. She was later recovered there by British forces on May 29, after the Battle of Goose Green.

The much needed cargo was uploaded by ARA *Forrest*, which made for Stanley. The coaster successfully completed *Monsunen's* relief mission on May 25. The action is thought to be the only naval encounter between armed surface ships in the war.

Source (edited): "http://en.wikipedia.org/wiki/Battle_of_Seal_Cove"

Battle of Two Sisters

The **Battle of Two Sisters** was an engagement of the Falklands War during the British advance towards the capital Stanley that took place from 11 to 12 June 1982.

Composition of forces

The British force consisted of 45 Commando (45 CDO), Royal Marines under Lieutenant-Colonel Andrew Whitehead (who later became a general) with support from six 105-mm guns of 29 Commando Regiment, Royal Artillery. 2 PARA was in reserve. Naval gunfire-support was provided by HMS Glamorgan's two 4.5-inch (114 mm) guns. The Argentinian force consisted of the 4th Infantry Regiment (RI 4). Command of Two Sisters was entrusted to Major Ricardo Cordón, second in command of RI 4, with the bulk of the defenders drawn from C Company with the 1st Platoon (Sub-Lieutenant Miguel Mosquera) and 2nd Platoon (Sub-Lieutenant Jorge Pérez Grandi) on the northern peak and the 3rd Platoon (Sub-Lieutenant Marcelo Llambias) on the southern peak and the 1st Platoon A Company (Sub-Lieutenant Juan Nazer) and Support Platoon (Second Lieutenant Luis Carlos Martella) on the saddle between the two peaks. Major Óscar Jaimet's B Company of the 6th Regiment (RI 6) acting as the local reserve occupied the saddle between Two Sisters and Mount Longdon.

Course of battle

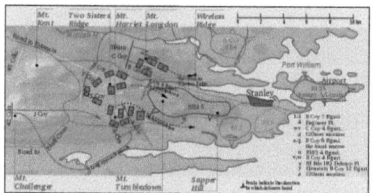

Night of 11 to 12 June, west of Stanley

On 4 June the three companies of 45 CDO advanced on Bluff Cove Peak, on the lower slopes of Mount Kent, and were able to occupy the feature without opposition and was met by patrols from the SAS. Enemy opposition was desultory but on the night of 29 May a fierce firefight developed in taking the two important hills, that were intended to form part of an Argentine Special Forces line. Captain Andrés Ferrero's patrol (3rd Assault Section, 602 Commando Company) made the base of Mount Kent but were then promptly pinned by machinegun and mortar fire. One Argentine NCO was wounded. Air Troop had two wounded from rifle fire. Probing attacks around the D Squadron positions continued throughout the night and at 11:00 am on 30 May, about 12 Argentine Commandos tried to get up the summit of Bluff Cove Peak, but were driven off by D Squadron SAS who killed two of the party, First Lieutenant Rubén Eduardo Márquez and Sergeant Óscar Humberto Blas. First Lieutenant Márquez and Sergeant Blas showed great personal courage and leadership in the contact and were subsequently awarded the Argentine Nation to the Valour in Combat Medal. During this contact the SAS suffered two casualties from grenades. The Argentine Commandos literally stumbled on a camp occupied by 15 SAS troopers, according to special forces historian Martin Arostegui who wrote *Twilight Warriors: Inside The World's Special Forces* (p. 205, Bloomsbury, 1995). Throughout 30 May Royal Air Force Harriers were active over Mount Kent. One of them in responding to a call for help from D Squadron attacked Mount Kent's eastern lower slopes and that led to its loss through small-arms fire.

A heavy mist hung over the Murrell River area and this assisted the 45 Commando Recce Troop to reach and sometimes penetrate the Argentine 3rd Platoon position under Sub-Lieutenant Marcelo Llambias. Marine Andrew Tubb of Recce Troop was on these patrols:

We were actually inside the Argentine position, so we ended up shelling ourselves. We did a lot of patrols up to Two Sisters ... that time [6 June] we pepper-potted [fire and maneuver] for about 400 metres to get out [the 3rd Platoon sergeant, Ramón Valdez, had launched a counterambush], through the Argy lines firing 66 [mm] rockets to fight through and regroup. We got artillery again to smoke us out. It took us well over an hour to get away and it seemed like a few minutes. We killed seventeen of them [two Army privates and three Sappers of a Marine minelaying party were actually killed], and all we had was one bloke with a flesh wound.

—Robin Neillands, *By Sea & Land: The Story of the Royal Marine Commandos*, p. 402, Cassell Military Paperbacks, 2000

For his patrol action, Lieutenant Chris Fox received the Military Cross. In general terms, the Argentines were thoroughly entrenched, about 6000 metres or less across a no-man's-land. The Argentine positions were mined and patrolled heavily.

At about 2.10 am local time on 10 June a strong 45 Commando fighting patrol probed the 3rd Platoon position. In the ensuing fight Special Forces Sergeants M. Cisneros and R. Acosta were killed; two more Argentine Special Forces lying in ambush for the Royal Marines were wounded. The British military historian Bruce Quarrie wrote later:

A constant series of patrols was undertaken at night to scout out and harass the enemy. Typical was the patrol sent out in the early hours of the morning of 10 June. Lieutenant David Stewart of X-Ray Company, 45 Commando, had briefed his men during the previous afternoon, and by midnight they were ready. Heavily armed, with two machine-guns per section plus 66 mm rocket launchers and 2-inch mortars, the Troop moved off stealthily into the moonlit night towards a ridge some

4 km away where Argentine movement had been observed. Keeping well spaced out because of the good visibility, they moved across the rocky ground using the numerous shell holes for cover, and by 04.00 [1 am local time] were set to cross the final stretch of open ground in front of the enemy positions. Using a shallow stream for cover, they moved up the slope and deployed into position among the rocks in front of the Argentine trenches. With the help of a light-intensifying night scope, they could see sentries moving about. Suddenly, an Argentine machine-gun opened fire and the Marines launched a couple of flares from their mortar, firing back with their own machine-guns and rifles. Within seconds three Argentine soldiers and two Marines were dead. Other figures could be seen running on the hill to the left, and four more Argentine soldiers fell to the accuracy of the Marines' fire. By this time, the Argentine troops further up the slope were wide awake, and a hail of fire forced the Marines to crouch in the shelter of the rocks. The situation was becoming decidedly unhealthy and Lieutenant Stewart decided to retire, with the objective of killing and harassing the enemy well and truly accomplished. However, a machine-gun to the Marines' right was pouring fire over their getaway route, and Stewart sent his veteran Sergeant, Jolly, with a couple of other men to take it out [They knew they were cut off with what looked a poor chance of escape. In these circumstances any panic or break in morale and the game was up]. After a difficult approach with little cover, there was a short burst of fire and the Argentine machine-gun fell silent. Leapfrogging by sections, the Troop retreated to the stream, by which time the Argentine fire was falling short and there were no further casualties.

—Bruce Quarrie, *The Worlds Elite Forces, pp.53-54*, Octopus Books Limited, 1985

Major Aldo Rico, commander of the 602 Commando Company himself had a lucky escape when an enemy rocket exploded uncomfortably close. Sadly for 45, on the night of 9–10 June there was an unfortunate mistake made in the dark and friendly fire was exchanged resulting in British casualties.

Captain Ian Gardiner's X-Ray Company spearheaded the attack on Two Sisters, accompanied by the Unit's Commando trained chaplain, the Revd Wynne Jones RN. Lieutenant James Kelly's 1 Troop took the western third of the spineback on the southern peak of Two Sisters (Long Toenail) with no fighting taking place. However at 11:30 pm local time (see No Picnic, p. 131), Lieutenant David Stewart's 3 Troop ran up against a very determined defence on the spineback and were unable to get forward. Beaten from their attempt to dislodge the Argentine 3rd Platoon, Lieutenant Chris Caroe's 2 Troop threw themselves at the platoon but the attack was dispersed with the help of artillery fire. For three or four hours X Ray Company were pinned down on the slopes of the mountain. Naval gunfire ripped back and forth across the mountain, but the Argentines held the Royal Marines off. Colonel Andrew Whitehead realized that a single company could not hope to secure Two Sisters without massive casualties, and brought up the battalion's two other companies.

At about 12:30 am local time (see No Picnic, p. 132) Yankee and Zulu Companies attacked the northern peak (Summer Days) and after a very hard two hour fight against two platoons and despite heavy machinegun and mortar fire, succeeded in capturing 'Summer Days'. The Z Company platoon commander, Lieutenant Clive Dytor, won the Military Cross by rallying his 8 Troop and leading it forward at bayonet point to take Summer Days. Yankee Company then advanced to attack the final objective capturing all of its objective all the way to the eastern end of Two Sisters. Second Lieutenant Aldo Eugenio Franco and his RI 6 platoon successfully prevented Yankee Company from attacking C Company as it withdrew from Two Sisters. Private Oscar Ismael Poltronieri who held up Yankee Company with accurate shooting with his rifle and a machinegun, was awarded the Argentine Nation to the Heroic Valour in Combat Cross (CHVC), the highest Argentine decoration for bravery. (Source Martin Middlebrook, *The Fight For The Malvinas*, Leo Cooper Paperbacks, 2003)

The next morning Colonel Andrew Whitehead looked in wonderment at the strength of the positions the enemy had abandoned. 'With fifty Royals,' he said, "I could have died of old age holding this place.' (Max Hastings, *Going To The Wars,* p. 363, Macmillan 2000) Although the British battalion seemed at the time to have had an easy victory, those actually engaged with the enemy platoons would have been unlikely to agree.

Some British writers were highly critical of the 6th Infantry Regiment's 'B' Company who, they claimed, withdrew in a disorderly manner from frontline positions at the opening of the battle, although this seems to have little foundation. Indeed, the company withdrew in good order, according to Spanish-speaking warrant officer attached to 3 Commando Brigade Headquarters in the fighting. The Argentine Army Official Report on the war recommended Major Oscar Jaimet and CSM Jorge Pitrella of the 6th Regiment's B Company for an MVC (Argentine Nation to the Valour in Combat Medal) for their conduct of their fighting withdrawal and subsequent behaviour on Tumbledown (this was later granted to Major Jaimet, Pitrella was awarded the Argentine Army to Military Merit Medal).

Sergeant-Major George Meachin of Yankee Company, would later praise the fighting abilities and spirit of the Argentine defenders:

" We came under lots of effective fire from 0.50 caliber machine guns ...At the same time, mortars were coming down all over us, but the main threat was from those machinegunners who could see us in the open because of the moonlight. There were three machineguns and we brought down constant and " effective salvoes of our own artillery fire on to them directly, 15 rounds at a time. There would be a pause, and they'd come back at us again. So we had to do it a second time, all over their positions. There'd be a pause, then 'boom, boom, boom,' they'd come back at us again. Conscripts don't do this, babies don't do this, men who are badly led and of low morale don't do this. They were good steadfast troops. I rate them.

Hugh Bicheno described the moonscape of devastation:
Although Wireless Ridge and the saddle between Tumbledown and William are still heavily scarred, even after more than twenty years the beaten zone between the Two Sisters bear the most eloquent witness to the awesome power of the British artillery, which fired 1,500 shells at the Two Sisters that night. The still-churned area occupied by Nazer's platoon in particular leaves one in no doubt why they decamped immediately, while the saddle itself is dimpled with craters, testimony to the tenacity of Martella's HMGs and mortars.

—Hugh Bicheno, *Razor's Edge: The Unofficial History of the Falklands War*, p. 242, Weidenfeld & Nicolson, 2006

With the telephone lines to the command post in shreds, Llambias-Pravaz led his men to join M Company 5th Marine Infantry Battalion on Sapper Hill.

The X-Ray Company Marines were in awe of the Argentines in the depleted 3rd Platoon who had put up such determined resistance, and their company commander in the book *Above All, Courage* (Above all, courage: the Falklands front line : first-hand accounts, Max Arthur, p. 289, Sidwick & Jackson, 1985) later said:

" A hard cadre of some twenty men had stayed behind and fought, and they were brave men. Those who stayed and fought had something. I for one would not wish to face my Marines in battle. "

A lone rifleman on Long Toenail held out long after resistance had ended on the mountain. There was a humorous moment when the Revd. Wynne Jones was challenged by the Marines and called out that he was 45 Commandos' padre and had forgotten the password.

Casualties

Seven Royal Marine Commandos and one Marine from 59 Independent Commando Squadron, Royal Engineers were killed taking Two Sisters. Another 17, including platoon commanders (Lieutenants Fox, Dunning and Davies) were wounded. Some 20 Argentines died in the first eleven days of June and the night of the battle, with another 54 taken prisoner.

HMS Glamorgan who was providing NGS stayed in her position to support the Royal Marine Commandos who were pinned down and there is no doubt that the County-class destroyer saved many lives. Glamorgan stayed past the time she was meant to leave and was hit by a land based Exocet missile, thirteen crew were killed as a result of this attack.

Awards received

For the bravery shown in the attack on Two Sisters, men from 45 Commando were awarded one DSO, three Military Crosses, one DCM and four Military Medals. A commando from 29 Commando received a Military Medal as did a man from the M&AW Cadre.
Source (edited): "http://en.wikipedia.org/wiki/Battle_of_Two_Sisters"

Battle of Wireless Ridge

The **Battle of Wireless Ridge** was an engagement of the Falklands War which took place on the night of 13 June and 14 June 1982, between British and Argentine forces during the advance towards the Argentine-occupied capital of the Falklands Stanley. Wireless Ridge was one of seven strategic hills within five miles of Stanley at 51°40′14″S 57°55′55″W that had to be taken in order for the city to be approached. The attack was successful, and the entire Argentine force on the Islands surrendered later that day.

The British force consisted of 2nd Battalion, The Parachute Regiment, a troop of the Blues & Royals, with two FV101 Scorpion and two FV107 Scimitar light tanks, as well as artillery support from two batteries of 29 Commando Regiment Royal Artillery and naval gunfire support provided by HMS *Ambuscade*'s 4.5-in gun. The Argentine force consisted of the 7th Infantry Regiment and detachments from other units.

Background

After heavy losses during the Battle of Goose Green, including their commander, Lieutenant Colonel Jones, command of 2 Para passed to Lieutenant-Colonel David Chaundler, who was in England at the time of the battle. Chaundler flew to Ascension Island on a Vickers VC10 and then to the Falklands on a C-130 Hercules that was dropping supplies by parachute. Chaundler jumped out into the sea, where he was picked up by helicopter and eventually delivered to HMS *Hermes* for a briefing with Admiral Woodward and then to Major General Jeremy Moore's headquarters. Four days after Goose Green, Chaundler joined 2 Para. After debriefing the battalion's officers about Goose Green and the events following, he vowed that 2 Para would never again go into action without fire support.

From Fitzroy, 2 Para were moved by helicopter to Bluff Cove Peak where they were held in reserve. The first line of hills, the Two Sisters, Mount Longdon and Mount Harriet, were taken. Three other hills were then slated to be captured: Mount Tumbledown by the Scots Guards, Mount William by the Ghurkhas and Wireless Ridge by 2

Para. The final phase of 3 Commando Brigade's campaign, a battle for Stanley, would follow capture of these hills. On the morning of 13 June, it became clear that the attacks on Tumbledown had been successful. So, 2 Para marched around the back of Mount Longdon to take up their positions for the assault on Wireless Ridge. As the action was expected to be concluded quickly, they took only their weapons and as much ammunition as possible, leaving most other gear behind in the camp. On Bluff Cove Peak, the Battalion's mortars and heavy machine guns were attacked by Argentine A-4 Skyhawks, which delayed their planned move forward, although they suffered no casualties.

Initial assault

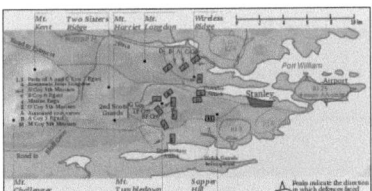

Final Actions, 13 to 14 June 1982

In the closing hours of the 13 June, D Coy began the attack, advancing upon 'Rough Diamond' hill north-west of Mount Longdon. It had been hit by an intense barrage from British guns, from land and sea. In the preceding 12 hours, British artillery had fired 6,000 rounds with their 105 mm pieces, and as they began their push, they were further backed by naval fire and the 76 and 30 mm guns mounted on the light tanks. The approximately eighty casualties sustained by 2 Para two weeks earlier at the Battle of Goose Green (including the loss of their commanding officer) had induced them not to take any unnecessary chances the second time around.

When D Coy reached the hill, they found that the Argentine *compañia* C of the 7th Infantry Regiment had withdrawn due to the heavy bombardment. As Major Philip Neame's D Coy started to consolidate their position, the Argentine 7th Regiment launched a series of heavy recoilless rifle, rocket and mortar attacks on Mount Longdon causing casualties to the 3rd Parachute Battalion of the Parachute Regiment (Jolly, 1983; p. 138).

With this massive fire support A and B Coys were convinced the enemy on Apple Pie were defeated, and began to advance confidently forward, but they met fierce resistance when they left their trenches. They came under heavy machine-gun fire and a massive retaliation was initiated by the British machine-gunners and the guns of the Blues and Royals light tanks.

One Mount Longdon survivor from 3 Para recalled the British attack in Hugh McManners' *The Scars of War* (1994) which was initially repulsed by the Argentines:

" They tried going over the top first, but the incoming fire was too heavy so they went back behind the peat and waited for more artillery to soften them up. "

(McManners, 1994)

The Argentine defenders there eventually withdrew in the face of such withering fire and A and B Coys took their objective. By this stage of the battle, there were not many Argentine officers left. The Forward Artillery Observation Officer (Major Guillermo Nani), the Operations Officer (Captain Carlos Ferreyra) and the *compañia* A and C commanders (Captains Jorge Calvo and Hugo García) and at least three senior platoon commanders (First Lieutenants Antonio Estrada, Jorge Guidobono, Ramon Galíndez-Matienzo) were wounded. C Coy then moved down from their northern start line to advance to a position east of Wireless Ridge where they found a platoon position to be unoccupied.

Final assault

D Coy then began the final assault from the western end of Wireless Ridge, under the cover of heavy fire from HMS *Ambuscade*'s 4.5 inch gun, tanks, twelve 105 mm artillery guns, several mortar pieces and anti-tank rockets. Earlier Argentine GHQ had sent the dismounted 10th Panhard armoured car squadron to make a reconnaissance foray into the western rocks of Wireless Ridge. Captain Rodrigo Soloaga was particularly effective in persuading his men to engage the light tanks, Milan Platoon and the Machinegun Platoon on Apple Pie while the 7th Regiment's HQ sorted themselves out. In two hours the cavalry unit suffered five killed and about fifty wounded. The British tankmen were so sickened by the slaughter that they held their fire as the walking wounded stumbled back to Moody Brook and stretcher-bearers tried to find the seriously wounded.

Major Neame's D Coy took the first half of the objective relatively easily but upon advancing to the second half, came under fierce attack from Major Guillermo Berazay's *compañia* A of the 3rd Regiment which had tried to move forward to Mount Longdon during the fighting two nights earlier but had only reached Moody Brook valley. Private Patricio Pérez, who had just left school, recalled the unnerving experience of 66 mm rockets coming straight at them like undulating fireballs. He believed he shot a British Paratrooper, possibly 12 Platoon's commander, and became enraged when he heard that his friend Private Horacio Benítez of his platoon had been shot. The platoon of 2nd Lieutenant Víctor Rodriguez Pérez of Major Guillermo Berazay's *compañia* A in fact closed with the British 12 Platoon, under the command of Lieutenant Jonathan Page (following the death of Lieutenant Barry at Goose Green). The fight surged back and forth. Lieutenant Page managed to hold the line, but only just. Major-General John Dutton Frost of the British Army describes the resulting attack on 12 Platoon:

" For two very long hours the company remained under pressure. Small-arms fire mingled with all types of HE [high explosive rifle-grenades] fell in and around 12 Platoon's position as the men crouched in the abandoned enemy sangars and in shell holes. "

(Frost, 1983)

Major Neame's officers and NCOs

rallied the men to capture the final part of their objective and in the face of heavy fire, the Argentines having run out of ammunition broke and retreated.

The battle was not over yet. Some 200 Wireless Ridge survivors had been rallied by the 10th Brigade Operations Officer, Major Eugenio Dalton to form under heavy gunfire a last-ditch defensive line in front of the now silenced guns of the 4th Airborne Artillery Group near the racecourse. Near the church in Stanley, intent on helping Berazay, Major Carrizo-Salvadores, 2IC of the 7th Regiment, helped by the chaplain Father José Fernández, mustered about 50 Wireless Ridge survivors and led them on a bayonet charge, with the soldiers chanting their famous 'Malvinas March', but were stopped by heavy artillery and machine-gun fire. ("Razor's Edge" Hugh Bicheno pg. 312)

The Paras were momentarily alarmed and watched surprised, with one British officer describing it as 'quite a sporting effort, but one without a sporting chance'. ("Operation Corporate" Martin Middlebrook pg. 371)

2 Para had suffered three dead and eleven wounded. The Argentines suffered approximately twenty-five dead, about 125 wounded (mainly by airburst rounds rather than direct shots) and about fifty were taken prisoner.

For the bravery shown at Wireless Ridge, 2 Para was awarded three Military Crosses, one Military Medal and one Distinguished Conduct Medal. 29 Commando was awarded one Military Cross.

Source (edited): "http://en.wikipedia.org/wiki/Battle_of_Wireless_Ridge"

Bluff Cove Air Attacks

The **Fitzroy Air Attacks** occurred 8 June 1982, during the Falklands War. British troop transport ships were bombed by the Argentine Air Force (FAA) whilst unloading, with significant damage and casualties.

Background

By 1 June, British forces on the Falkland Islands were bolstered by the arrival of 5,000 new troops of the 5th Infantry Brigade. Major General Jeremy Moore now had sufficient force to start planning a full scale assault on Port Stanley.

Advance parties of 2 Para moved forward and occupied Fitzroy and Bluff Cove, when it was discovered to be clear of Argentine forces. Units of the Welsh Guards and Scots Guards were sent in to support them. After the sinking of the transport *Atlantic Conveyor* there was only one British troop carrying helicopter available, an RAF CH-47 Chinook. Therefore, supplies and reinforcements would have to be transported by sea.

Air strikes

While unloading on 8 June, the British ships were attacked by waves of A-4 Skyhawks from the 5th Air Brigade, each of them loaded with three 500 lb retarding tail bombs of Spanish design. At approximately 14:00 local time the ships RFA *Sir Tristram* and RFA *Sir Galahad* were badly damaged by five A-4Bs of *Grupo 5*. At 16:50 a second wave, composed by four A-4Bs of *Grupo 5* hit a LCU from HMS *Fearless*, ferrying the vehicles of the 5th Brigade's headquarters from Darwin to Bluff Cove in Choiseul Sound with the loss of six of her crew. However, the Sea Harrier combat air patrol was already on scene and responded; three Skyhawks were shot down and their pilots, 1st Lt Danilo Bolzan, Lt Juan Arrarás, and Ensign Alfredo Vazquez, were killed. The fourth aircraft suffered combat damage and lost a large amount of fuel, but returned to the mainland, assisted by a KC-130 tanker. A third wave, by A-4Cs of *Grupo 4*, arrived minutes later and struck ground targets without visible success. In a separate incident, the frigate HMS *Plymouth* endured the sudden attack of six Dagger fighters of the 6th Air Brigade, which struck her with four 1,000-pound bombs. The warship sustained severe damage, although all the bombs were duds.

A total of 56 British servicemen were killed, and 150 wounded. BBC television cameras recorded images of Royal Navy helicopters hovering in thick smoke to winch survivors from the burning landing ships. These images were seen around the world. However, General Mario Menendez, commander of Argentine forces on the islands, was told that hundreds of men had been killed. He expected a drop in British morale, and their advance to slacken. *Sir Galahad* was damaged beyond repair, but her sister ship survived to be re-built post-war.

Aftermath

1° Lt. Carlos Cachón in 1982

Among the wounded was Simon Weston, who later featured in a BBC documentary showing his treatment for the appalling injuries he received. Weston endured 75 operations in 22 years, after 25% of his skin suffered third degree burns. In a subsequent documentary, filmed in Argentina, he met the pilot who bombed his ship, Captain Carlos Cachón. After a later visit of Cachón and his family to Weston's home in Liverpool, they have become great friends.

Carlos Cachón was born near Balcarce and raised in Mar del Plata, where he currently lives. He was awarded the honorific title of "Illustrious Citizen" by the Council of the city of Mar del Plata on 25 February 2010.

After the war, a memorial for the British soldiers killed in the attack was erected at Fitzroy. On 8 June 2007, Welsh Guards veterans of the Falklands War held a memorial for the Welsh Guards killed on board *Sir Galahad*. Source (edited): "http://en.wikipedia.org/wiki/Bluff_Cove_Air_Attacks"

Mount Kent Skirmish

The **Mount Kent Skirmish** occurred during the Falklands War on 30-31 May 1982 when an Argentine patrol from 602 Commando Company commanded by Captain Eduardo Villarruel ran into a British patrol from D Squadron 22nd Special Air Service on the slopes of Mount Kent. The British took control of the situation.

The Argentines are noted as to having passed out the radio message: "We are in trouble" and then forty minutes later: "There are English all around us... you had better hurry up".

The following night on 31 May, K Company of 42 Commando, Royal Marines arrived nearby. The sight of a night firefight in progress confronted them. The Marines quickly took cover and after the fire fight had died down Major Cedric Delves of D Squadron, 22 SAS appeared and assured them that all was well and that the SAS had destroyed an Argentine patrol.

One historian's account states the following:

" *The SAS finally managed to surround the main commando group, consolidating into a position near the peak, and ambushed them with one of those devastating, explosive onslaughts of automatic fire and GPMG fire for which the regiment is famous. On sighting the 2nd Assault Section, the SAS spread out and opened a sharp fire on the* Commandos from the cover of boulders. Within minutes, the Argentine patrol began to crumble as the Commandos came under fire from an enemy they couldn't even see. "We would have fought," said Captain Tomas Fernandez, "if we had seen anyone to fight with". One of the Argentine Commandos, Sergeant Alfredo Flores, was captured on Bluff Cove Peak and he stated later that he had been "left behind by his commander". "

Source (edited): "http://en.wikipedia.org/wiki/Mount_Kent_Skirmish"

Raid on Pebble Island

The **Raid on Pebble Island** took place on 14-15 May 1982 during the Falklands War. Pebble Island is part of the Falkland Islands.

Background

Immediately after the Argentines had seized the Falkland Islands they established a small airbase on Pebble Island using the local airstrip on which were based FMA IA 58 Pucará light ground attack aircraft and some T-34 Mentors. These reconnaissance aircraft could have compromised the Royal Navy's manoeuvres before its intended landing on East Falkland. Special Air Service elements, then embarked on HMS *Hermes*, were tasked with eliminating the threat, with naval support from the Type 22 frigate HMS *Broadsword* as *Hermes* defensive escort and the County class destroyer HMS *Glamorgan* to provide naval gunfire support with its Mark 6 4.5 inch gun. The Naval Gunfire Support Forward Observer (NGSFO) who was responsible for co-ordinating the naval gunfire support was Captain Chris Brown RA of 148 Battery 29 Commando Regiment Royal Artillery.

Initial intentions

Initial intentions were for a Squadron strength air insertion from *Hermes* using personnel from D Squadron, 22 Regiment. The raiding party would destroy the deployed aircraft, radar site, ground crew and the force protection garrison before helicopter exfiltration to return to the deck before daybreak.

Reconnaissance

Reconnaissance for the raid was conducted by personnel from the Boat Troop of D Squadron, conducting an infiltration by Klepper canoe. The patrol found that strong headwinds would increase the time taken to fly in from *Hermes* launch point, delaying time on target and reducing the available offensive window to 30 minutes, rather than the planned 90. In light of this information the planning emphasised the importance of destroying the aircraft as a priority, with support personnel as a secondary priority.

The raid

During the night of 14 May, two Westland Sea King HC4 helicopters of 846 Naval Air Squadron, part of the Commando Helicopter Force, departed with 45 members of D Squadron on board. The delivery point was 6 km (3.7 miles) from the airstrip on Pebble Island. Mountain Troop was tasked with the destruction of the Argentine aircraft, while the remaining personnel acted as a protection force, securing approaches to the airstrip, and forming an operational reserve. The raiding party unloaded over 100 L16 81mm Mortar bombs, explosive charges, and Rocket 66mm HEAT L1A1 Light Anti-tank Weapons to carry into the engagement zone from the helicopters, with each man in the raiding party carrying at least two mortar bombs. For small arms, M-16 rifles were used, some with underslung M203 grenade launchers. Approach navigation was conducted by a member of the Boat Troop who had carried out the reconnaissance.

As the raiding party approached the target they spotted an Argentine sentry but were not seen, allowing them to enter the target and lay charges on seven of the aircraft. Once all the aircraft had been prepared the raiding team opened fire on the aircraft with small arms and L1A1 rockets. All of the aircraft were damaged, with some having their undercarriages shot away. Following this cue *Glamorgan* began shelling the Argentine positions on the airfield using high-explosive rounds, hitting the ammunition dump and fuel stores.

The defending force did not engage until the entire raiding party had regrouped and were preparing to move out. One British soldier was hit and wounded while the raiding party returned fire using small arms and M203 grenade launchers, resulting in the death of the Argentine Commanding Officer (according to British assessments) and the suppression of any defensive effort.

The Argentine version states that their marines remained in shelters during the *Glamorgan* shelling, so they were unable to face the SAS in combat. The British wounded were the result of shrapnel from exploding charges settled by the Argentines under the airstrip in order to deny its use to the enemy. The blasts were triggered in the belief that the operation was a full-scale assault to take over the air base.

Exfiltration

The wounded man was hauled back to the recovery site with the raiding party reaching the aircraft by the required time for transportation back to *Hermes* before daybreak. The decision was made to proceed with exfiltration rather than returning to attack the defending force.

Aftermath

Assets destroyed during the raid totalled:
- Six FMA IA 58 Pucarás, *air force*.
- Four Turbo Mentor trainer/light attack aircraft, *navy*.
- One Short SC.7 Skyvan utility transport aircraft, *coast guard*.
- Destruction of the ammunition dump
- Destruction of the fuel dump

The raid was considered a complete success, reminiscent of the type of operation carried out by the SAS in the Second World War.

One of the officers involved, Captain Hamilton, was later killed in another SAS action near Port Howard.
Source (edited): "http://en.wikipedia.org/wiki/Raid_on_Pebble_Island"

Skirmish at Many Branch Point

On 10 June 1982, during the Falklands War, **Many Branch Point**, a ridge near Port Howard, in West Falkland, was the site of a minor skirmish between Argentine and British elite forces. The engagement ended with the death of the SAS patrol commander, Captain Gavin John Hamilton. This action was the only land engagement of British and Argentine forces on West Falkland during the Falklands War.

Background

While the 35 mm radar-guided and 20 mm antiaircraft guns in Port Stanley and Goose Green forced Sea Harrier and Harrier GR.3 to carry out air strikes from high altitude, the Argentine garrisons at West Falkland relied only on 12.7 mm machine guns for their own protection, which left them exposed to strafing and low-level bombing.

In order to reinforce these units, the Argentine command-in-chief deployed a special forces company, the 601, to Port Howard, then headquarters of the 5º Regiment of Infantry. The commandos were equipped with British-made, shoulder-fired Blowpipe missiles. After a 24-hours trip from Port Stanley, the company reached its destination.

Some days later, with the British landing at San Carlos bay still ongoing, the Argentine troops found their mark when they shot down a GR3 Harrier on a recce mission. The pilot, Flt. Lt. Jeffrey Glover, bailed out safely and was taken prisoner.

The Argentine garrison became isolated and the commandos orders were to collect information about enemy activity on the opposite coast of the Falkland Sound.

In the meantime, SAS patrols had been active around the main Argentine advance posts. On June 5, a 4-men party led by Captain Gavin John Hamilton moved as close as 2.5 km from the enemy to gather intelligence around Port Howard. Hamilton was an officer in the squadron that raided the air base at Pebble Island on May 16.

The action

On the morning of June 9, a routine reconnaissance patrol of the Argentine special forces, under the command of First Lieutenant José Martiniano Duarte marched to Many Branch point, a hill located 5 miles to the north of Howard. Previously, an observation post had been deployed on Mount Rosalie, but it had been compromised due to the British presence. Nevertheless, the Commandos managed to withdraw without detection. The squad was originally composed of 9 men; by the afternoon, with no enemy in sight, five men returned to base, while the other four remained on the ridge. From this position, they were able to observe that a British airfield had been built near San Carlos.

British sources state that Captain Hamilton was 'heavily outnumbered' in the resulting action which would appear to contradict Moreno's account.

The following day, while in position, Duarte heard some voices behind a rocky formation. The patrol gathered at the entrance of cave-shaped rocks, assuming that either a British section was hidden there, or simply they were local shepherds.

Suddenly, a dark-skinned man, wearing a balaclava, was spotted. Initially there was some hesitation as some of the man's clothing resembled Argentine uniform, Duarte cried: "*Argentinos o Ingleses?*" (*Argentine or English?*). After a short silence, Lieutenant Duarte ordered: "Hands up, hands up!". The response was a burst of fire, which bounced off the stones in front of him. During the engagement, an Argentine Sergeant launched two grenades, in response a British 40 mm grenade exploded a few meters behind the Commandos. Under the weight of fire from Duarte's patrol the British patrol attempted to withdraw down the hill. The commander, Captain John Hamilton, attempted to cover his comrade, but was hit and killed by automatic fire and a rifle-launched grenade. The other soldier surrendered shortly after.

The prisoner was a signal corps member of Goan origin, Corporal Charlie Fonseca. Although Captain Hamilton wore no rank or insignia (as is SAS practise), he was identified by his dog tag. Also found upon the men were a radio, an M16 and an AR-15 rifle, a beacon, cartography and a communications code. The other two soldiers of Hamilton's party managed to escape and were later rescued by friendly forces.

Aftermath

That night witnessed the inaccurate shelling carried out by British frigates on Port Howard. It led to speculation among Argentine officers that the mission of Hamilton was to act as Naval Gunfire Support Forward Observer (NGSFO).

The autopsy revealed that Hamilton was killed by a 7.62 mm shot in his back. Another bullet hit his arm. He was buried at Port Howard, along with an Argentine conscript who died of starvation, a clear signal of the hopeless scenario for the troops in West Falkland. Hamilton's grave can still be seen up the hill from Port Howard.

When the Argentine Commander of Port Howard was interrogated after the Argentine surrender, he asked that 'the SAS Captain' be decorated for his actions as he was 'the most courageous man I have ever seen' In the event Captain Hamilton was posthumously awarded the Military Cross.

Source (edited): "http://en.wikipedia.org/wiki/Skirmish_at_Many_Branch_Point"

Skirmish at Top Malo House

The **Skirmish at Top Malo House** was fought on 31 May 1982 during the Falklands War, between 1st section Argentine Special Forces from 602 Commando Company and a patrol formed from staff and students of the British Mountain and Arctic Warfare Cadre, a training unit of the Royal Marines placed under Operational Control of 3 Commando Brigade for Operation Corporate.

Background

Captain Rod Boswell of the Royal Marines Mountain and Arctic Warfare Cadre and eighteen of his men undertook the task which originated from a report made on 27 May by a four man patrol from the Cadre sited in an Observation Post on Bull Hill. The four man patrol had established the OP on 21 May as one of a number of small reconnaissance teams who were the eyes and ears of the Brigade.

Prelude

The four man patrol were well forward on Bull Hill on the route from Teal Inlet to Stanley. They had just reported back to say that this may be the last message because two Argentine UH-1 helicopters were hovering over the OP. The helicopters flew off in the direction of Mount Simon; however, the sergeant commanding the team believed that the aircraft had probably dropped off Argentine Special Forces on the lower slopes of Mount Simon. The subsequent message back to Brigade Headquarters alerted the staff to the threat of Argentine Special Forces sited on high ground on the approaches to Teal Inlet and beyond. It would be the task of Captain Boswell and his team to eliminate the Argentine patrol at Top Malo.

During 29 May the radio operator of the Argentine patrol, after trying all morning, suddenly managed to get a message through to 10th Brigade HQ, that there was an air corridor to and from San Carlos to Mount Kent. Contact was immediately lost, never to be re-established. The commander of the patrol was Captain Jose Arnobio Vercesi, commander of the 1st Assault Section, 602 Commando Company. The patrol was formed by 8 men of the first section plus two soldiers with Blowpipe missile. There was also one medic, First Sergeant Pedrozo, whilst First Sergeant Helguero from 601 Commando Company was the scout.

On the evening of 30 May Captain Boswell received a message from one of the patrols, in an observation post on the lower slopes of Mount Simon, that they had just seen two Argentine UH-1 helicopters deliver a patrol of about sixteen men at Top Malo House, a deserted shepherd's house just 400 metres (440 yd) from their position. They also reported hearing several other helicopters in the vicinity. It was already getting dark, which ruled out a Harrier GR3 strike against the house, and the location was out of range of the British artillery. Consequently, the British planned an assault following insertion by helicopter early on the morning of 31 May, landing in dead ground about 1,000 metres (1,100 yd) away from the house, and attacking the house.

Battle

Embarked in a Sea King HC4 of 846 Naval Air Squadron, attached to the Royal Marines, the team was loaded with sufficient supplies and ammunition to last a week in the field. The overloaded helicopter took off on a 45 km flight, depositing the team on exactly the right spot to allow disembarkation for the short transit to the target. A seven-man fire team moved off to the left to take up a position 150m away from Top Malo House to provide support fire for the twelve-man assault group led by Boswell. There was a significant risk of compromise as the team was wearing dark uniforms against the snow, leading to the possibility of visual detection by sentries. Unknown to the British, the Argentines heard the helicopter's flying and accelerated actions to take their equipment and leave the house.

Boswell initiated the engagement about two hours after dawn, following an order to fix bayonets, by firing a green flare into the air. This was the signal for the support group to fire six M72 LAW 66mm light anti-armour rockets at the house. As the first rocket was fired an Argentine sentry (Lieutenant Ernesto Espinosa, who was the Argentine sniper in the patrol) moved to the window of the upper floor, being immediately shot and wounded by a Corporal Groves in the support team, who was armed with a L42A1 sniper rifle. Lieutenant Horacio Losito, who was the second in command of the section, says that Lieutenant Espinosa raised the alarm and at the same time opened fire on the approaching British troops allowing the Argentines to get out of the house.

One of the British members of the fireteam was close enough for his 66mm LAW rocket to be hit by Espinosa. As the rockets hit the house it burst into flames. Boswell and his group charged forward, halted, fired two more rockets, and then charged again. The Argentines ran from the house to a nearby stream bed about 200 m away, firing as they ran. Lieutenant Espinosa on the top floor was killed by a 66mm rocket while Sergeant Mateo Sbert was shot dead as he gave covering fire as the remaining Argentines exited the single door. Two British personnel, a sergeant and a corporal, were hit and wounded. The ammunition stacked inside the house exploded. As the British assault group moved forward the smoke from the burning building provided screening from the accurate fire from the Argentine commandos firing from the stream bed.

The firefight went on for about forty-five minutes. With ammunition running very low and most of the patrol killed or wounded Captain Vercesi elected to surrender. Lieutenant Espinosa and Sergeant Sbert were awarded the posthumous Argentine Nation to the Heroic Valour in Combat Cross for this action.

Aftermath

Two Argentines were killed, six wounded and another four taken prisoner, with three of the British force having been wounded. After the battle Captain Boswell comment to the Argentine Commander was: "Never in a house...".

Unknown to the British the entire assault had been watched by members of *Red de Observadores del Aire* or ROA (the Argentine Air Force forward deployed ground observation teams) on Malo Hill and Mount Simon. In fact, a four man patrol led by Lieutenant Hadow watched the action from a nearby position just on the other side of Malo river. Fourteen R.O.A. personnel from these positions surrendered to 3 Para the next day.

Source (edited): "http://en.wikipedia.org/wiki/Skirmish_at_Top_Malo_House"

1982 invasion of the Falkland Islands

On 2 April 1982, **Argentine forces mounted amphibious landings of the Falkland Islands** (Spanish: *Islas Malvinas*). The invasion involved an initial defence force organised by the Falkland Islands' Governor Sir Rex Hunt giving command to Major Mike Norman of the Royal Marines, the landing of Lieutenant-Commander Guillermo Sánchez-Sabarots' Amphibious Commandos Group on Mullet Creek, the attack on Moody Brook barracks, the engagement between the amphibious personnel carriers of Hugo Santillán and Bill Trollope marines east of Stanley, and the battle and final surrender of Government House. It marked the beginning of the Falklands War.

Defence

Governor Sir Rex Hunt was informed by the British Government of a possible Argentine invasion on 1 April. At 3:30 pm that day he received a telegram from the Foreign and Commonwealth Office stating:

We have apparently reliable evidence that an Argentine task force could be assembling off Stanley at dawn tomorrow. You will wish to make your dispositions accordingly.

Forces involved

The Governor summoned the two senior Royal Marines officers of Naval Party 8901 to Government House in Stanley to discuss the options for defending the Falklands. He said during the meeting, "Sounds like the buggers mean it", remaining composed despite the seriousness of the situation that the islands faced.

Major Mike Norman was given overall command of the Marines due to his seniority, while Major Gary Noott became the military advisor to Governor Hunt. The total strength was 68 Marines and 11 sailors, which was greater than would normally have been available because the garrison was in the process of changing over. Both the replacements and the troops preparing to leave were in the Falklands at the time of the invasion. This was decreased to 57 when 22 Royal Marines embarked aboard the Antarctic patrol ship HMS *Endurance* to observe Argentine soldiers based at South Georgia. The Royal Navy, on the other hand, states that a total of 85 marines were present at Stanley. Their numbers were reinforced by at least 25 Falkland Islands Defence Force (FIDF) members. Graham Bound, an islander who lived through the Argentine occupation, reports in his book *Falkland Islanders At War* that the higher figure of approximately 40 (both serving and past) members of the FIDF reported for duty at their Drill Hall. Their commanding officer, Major Phil Summers, tasked the volunteer militiamen with guarding such key points as the telephone exchange, the radio station and the power station. Skipper Jack Sollis, on board the civilian coastal ship *Forrest* operated his boat as an improvised radar screen station off Stanley. Two other civilians, former Marine Jim Alister and a Canadian citizen, Bill Curtiss, also offered their services to the Governor.

Operation *Rosario*

The Argentine amphibious operation began in the late evening of Thursday 1 April, when the destroyer ARA *Santisima Trinidad* disembarked special naval forces south of Stanley. The bulk of the Argentine forces was to land some hours later from the amphibious warfare ship ARA *Cabo San Antonio* near the airport, on a beach previously marked by frogmen from the submarine ARA *Santa Fe*.

The operation had been called *Azul* (Blue) during the planning stage, but it was finally renamed *Rosario* (Rosary).

ARA *Santa Fe*

The very first move of Operation *Rosario* was the reconnaissance of Port William by the submarine ARA *Santa Fe* and the landing of 14 members of the tactical divers group near Cape Pembroke, including the commander of this elite unit, Captain Cufré. The recce mission began as early as 31 March, when the trawler *Forrest* was spotted through the periscope at 10:00 PM off Port Stanley. The next day, the *Santa Fe* learned that the authorities in Stanley were aware of the Argentine intentions, so a change of plans was in order. Instead of landing right on Pembroke, the commandos would initially take a beach near Menguera Point, south of Kidney Island. They left the *Santa Fe* at 1:40 PM. From the beach, they headed towards Pembroke peninsula in Zodiac boats. They reached Yorke Bay at 4:30 AM of 2 April. After planting beacons for the main landing, they took over the airstrip and the lighthouse without resistance. Argentine sources claim that they captured a few prisoners. This team was later given the task of gathering and taking in custody the Royal Marines in their flight out of the islands after the British surrender.

Attack on Moody Brook barracks

On the night of 1/2 April, the destroyer ARA *Santísima Trinidad* halted 500 metres off Mullet Creek and lowered 21 Gemini assault craft into the water. They contained 84 special forces troopers of Lieutenant-Commander Guillermo Sánchez-Sabarots' 1st Amphibious Commandos Group and a small party under Lieutenant-Commander Pedro Giachino, who was normally 2IC of the 1st Marine Infantry Battalion, that was to capture Government House. The Argentine Rear Admiral Jorge Allara, through a message radioed from *Santisima Trinidad*, had requested to Rex Hunt a peaceful surrender, but the proposal was rejected.

Giachino's party had the shortest distance to go: two and a half miles due north. Moody Brook Barracks, the destination of the main party, was six miles away, over rough Falklands terrain. Lieutenant-Commander Sánchez-Sabarots, in the book *The Argentine Fight for The Falklands*, describes the main party's progress in the dark:

Two Argentine noncommissioned officers, members of the Amphibious Commandos party that seized Moody Brook

It was a nice night, with a moon, but the cloud covered the moon for most of the time. It was very hard going with our heavy loads; it was hot work. We eventually became split up into three groups. We only had one night sight; the lead man, Lieutenant Arias had it. One of the groups became separated when a vehicle came along the track we had to cross. We thought it was a military patrol. Another group lost contact, and the third separation was caused by someone going too fast. This caused my second in command, Lieutenant Bardi, to fall. He suffered a hairline fracture of the ankle and had to be left behind with a man to help him. We were at Moody Brook by 5.30 a.m., just on the limits of the time planned, but with no time for the one hour's reconnaissance for which we had hoped.

The main party of Argentine Marines assumed that the Moody Brook Barracks contained sleeping Royal Marines. The barracks were quiet, although a light was on in the office of the Royal Marine commander. No sentries were observed, and it was a quiet night, apart from the occasional animal call. Lieutenant-Commander Sánchez-Sabarots could hear nothing of any action at Government House, nor from the distant landing beaches; nevertheless, he ordered the assault to begin. Lieutenant-Commander Sánchez-Sabarots continues his account:

It was still completely dark. We were going to use tear-gas to force the British out of the buildings and capture them. Our orders were not to cause casualties if possible. That was the most difficult mission of my career. All our training as commandos was to fight aggressively and inflict maximum casualties on the enemy. We surrounded the barracks with machine-gun teams, leaving only one escape route along the peninsula north of Stanley Harbour. Anyone who did get away would not able to reach the town and reinforce the British there. Then we threw the gas grenades into each building. There was no reaction; the barracks were empty.

The noise of the grenades alerted Major

Norman to the presence of Argentines on the island, and he thus drove back to Government House. Realising that the attack was coming from Moody Brook, he ordered all troop sections to converge on the house to enable the defence to be centralised.

Although there were no Royal Marine witnesses to the assault, British descriptions of the state of Moody Brook barracks afterward contradict the Argentine version of events. After the action, some of the Royal Marines were allowed to return to barracks to collect personal items. Major Norman describes walls of the barracks as riddled with machine gun fire and bearing the marks of white phosphorus grenades—"a classic houseclearing operation".

Amphibious landing at Yorke Bay

ARA *Cabo San Antonio*

Argentine marines and APCs at Stanley, 2 April 1982

There was a more pressing action on the eastern edge of Stanley. Twenty US-built LVTP-7A1 Argentine tracked amphibious armoured personnel carriers from the 1st Amphibious Vehicles Battalion, carrying D and E Companies of the 2nd Marine Infantry Battalion (BIM-2) from Puerto Belgrano, had been landed from the tank landing ship ARA *Cabo San Antonio* at Yorke Bay, and were being watched by a section of Royal Marines under the command of Lieutenant Bill Trollope. The armoured column trundled along the Airport Road into Stanley, with three Amtracs (Numbers 05, 07 and 19) in the vanguard, and, near the Ionospheric Research Station, at exactly 7:15 am, was engaged by a section of Royal Marines with anti-tank rockets and machine guns. This from Lieutenant-Commander Hugo Santillán's official post-battle report:

We were on the last stretch of the road into Stanley. A machine-gun fired from one of the three white houses about 500 metres away and hit the right-hand Amtrac. The fire was very accurate. Then there were some explosions from a rocket launcher, but they were inaccurate, falling a long way from us. We followed our standard operating procedure and took evasive action. The Amtrac on the right returned fire and took cover in a little depression. Once he was out of danger, I told all three vehicles to disembark their men. I ordered the crew with the recoilless rifle to fire one round of hollow charge at the ridge of the roof of the house where the machine-gun was, to cause a bang but not an explosion. We were still following our orders not to inflict casualties. The first round was about a hundred metres short, but the second hit the roof. The British troops then threw a purple smoke grenade; I thought it was their signal to withdraw. They had stopped firing, so Commander Weinstabl started the movement of the two companies around the position. Some riflemen in one of the houses started firing then; that was quite uncomfortable. I couldn't pinpoint their location, but one of my other Amtracs could and asked permission to open up with a mortar which he had. I authorized this, but only with three rounds and only at the roofs of the houses. Two rounds fell short, but the third hit right in the centre of the roof; that was incredible. The British ceased firing then.

The Amtrac on the right manoeuvred itself off the road into a little depression and as it did so, disembarked the Marines inside out of view. This encouraged the Royal Marines to think that Marine Mark Gibbs had scored a direct hit on the passenger compartment of the APC.

Lieutenant Bill Trollope, with No. 2 Section, describes the action:

Six Armoured Personnel Carriers began advancing at speed down the Airport Road. The first APC was engaged at a range of about 200 to 250 metres. The first three missiles, two 84 mm and one 66 mm, missed. Subsequently one 66 mm fired by Marine Gibbs, hit the passenger compartment and one 84 mm Marines Brown and Betts hit the front. Both rounds exploded and no fire was received from that vehicle. The remaining five APCs which were about 600 to 700 metres away deployed their troops and opened fire. We engaged them with GPMG, SLR and sniper rifle [Sergeant Shepherd] for about a minute before we threw a white phosphorus smoke grenade and leap-frogged back to the cover of gardens. Incoming fire at that stage was fairly heavy, but mostly inaccurate.

Lieutenant Trollope and his men withdrew along Davis Street, running behind the houses with Argentine Marines in hot pursuit, and went to ground firing up the road when it became obvious they could not reach Government House.

Battle of Government House and surrender

One of the Amphibious Commandos after the fall of Stanley's Government House

Lying on a small hillock south of Government House, Lieutenant-Commander Pedro Giachino faced the difficulty of capturing this important objective with no radio and with a force of only sixteen men. He split his force into small groups, placing one on either side of the house and one at the rear. Unknown to them, the Governor's residence was the main concentration point of the Royal Marines, who outnumbered the Commandos by two to one. The first attack against this building came at 6.30 a.m., barely an hour before the Yorke Bay amphibious landing, when one of Giachino's platoons, led by Lieutenant Gustavo Lugo, started to exchange fire with the British troops inside the house. At the same time, Giachino himself, with four of his subordinates, entered the servants' annexe, believing it to be the rear entrance to the residence. Three Royal Marines, Corporals Sellen and Fleet and Marine Dorey, who were placed to cover the annexe, beat off the first attack. Giachino was hit instantly as he burst through the door, while Lieutenant Diego Garcia Quiroga was shot in the arm. The remaining three retreated to the maid's quarters. Giachino was not dead, but very badly wounded. An Argentine paramedic, Corporal Ernesto Urbina, attempted to get to Giachino but was wounded by a grenade. Giachino, seeing what had happened, pulled the pin from a hand grenade and threatened to use it. The Royal Marines then attempted to persuade the officer to get rid of the grenade so that they could give him medical treatment, but he refused, preventing them from reaching his position. After the surrender of the British forces at Government House, some three hours later, Giachino was taken to Stanley Hospital but died from loss of blood.

ARA *Granville*

At the Governor's office, Major Norman received a radio report from Corporal York's section, which was positioned at Camber peninsula, observing any possible Argentine ship entering Stanley Harbour.

The Corporal proceeded to report on three potential targets in sight and which should he engage first. *What are the targets?* the Major enquired. *Target number one is an aircraft carrier, target number two is a cruiser*, at which point the line went dead. Corporal York decided to withdraw his section and proceeded to booby trap their Carl Gustav recoilless rifle, before paddling their Gemini assault boat north across Port William. As he did so, York claimed an Argentine destroyer began pursuing them (the corvette ARA *Granville* according to Argentine sources). His initiative led to the Gemini reaching an anchored Polish fishing vessel, hiding the small assault boat under her shadow. They patiently waited for a chance, before moving to the shore and landing on a small beach.

Back at Government House, the Argentine commandos' pressure continued unabated. There is some evidence that their use of stun grenades and their continuous shift of firing positions during the battle led the Royal Marines inside to believe they were facing a company of marines and were hopelessly outnumbered. Actually, after the failure of Giachino's platoon to break into the residence, the British were surrounded by only a dozen elite troops. These men were under Lieutenant Lugo, Giachino's Second-in-Command. The Land Rovers used by the Royal Marines were disabled by automatic gunfire from the commandos. Governor Hunt called Patrick Watts (at the radio station, Radio Stanley), by telephone and said he believed the assaulting force to be the equivalent of a reinforced company:

We're staying put here, but we are pinned down. We can't move.(...) They must have 200 around us now. They've been throwing rifle grenades at us; I think there may be mortars, I don't know. They came along very quickly and very close, and then they retreated. Maybe they are waiting until the APCs [Amtracs] come along and they think they'll lose less casualties that way.

Consequently, Hunt decided to enter talks with Argentine commanders around 8 o'clock. The liaison was Vice-Commodore Hector Gilobert, the head in the islands of LADE, the Argentine government's airline company. Gilobert and a Governor's deputy went to the Argentine headquarters displaying a white flag. A de facto ceasefire was put in place at that time which was occasionally breached by small arms fire.

The Governor's envoys found the Argentine commanding post at Stanley's Town Hall. The Argentine chief accepted the British offer of a face to face meeting with Rex Hunt at his battered office.

Vice-Commodore Hector Gilobert on his way to Government House

Eight FIDF members taken prisoners by Amphibious Commandos heading to Government House

An Argentine amphibious vehicle from BIM-2 patrolling Stanley

While the negotiations were still going on, another incident occurred inside the residence. Three Argentine survivors of the first skirmish along the compound inadvertently alerted Major Noott to their presence, while they had been preparing to leave their hiding place. The Major fired his Sterling submachine gun into the ceiling of the maid's room. According to British reports, the stunned commandos tumbled down the stairs, laying their weapons on the ground. They became the first Argentine prisoners of war of the Falklands War, albeit by then, Governor Hunt had already been in contact with Argentine officials negotiating the terms of surrender. The version of the commander of these men, Captain Cufré, who was then at Stanley airport, is that his three subordinates kept their fighting position right to the end of the hostilities. Admiral Busser, commander in chief of the operation, states that a cease fire was already in place when the three commandos, after realising that the battle was coming to a close and that any loss of life at the time would be futile, laid down their arms to the marines in order to assist the wounded. Just a few minutes after this event, Government house had capitulated.

Meanwhile, the Royal Marines in the House saw the approaching Amtracs that had been engaged earlier by Lieutenant Trollope and his section. The vehicles pushed on toward Moody Brook to link up with Sánchez-Sabarots forces. His amphibious commandos were plodding slowly along the road to reinforce their colleagues besieging Government House after taking some prisoners near the racecourse. Major Norman had earlier advised Rex Hunt that the Royal Marines and the Governor could break out to the countryside and set up a 'seat of government' elsewhere, but when he finally met the commander-in-chief of the Argentine operations, Admiral Busser, he agreed to surrender his troops to the now overwhelming Argentine forces at 9:30 AM.

After the surrender, the Royal Marines and the members of the FIDF were then herded onto the playing fields. Pictures and film were taken of the British prisoners arranged face-down on the ground. This was probably an attempt by Argentina to demonstrate the lack of British casualties, but it backfired: The images galvanised the British public when they were broadcast on television and increased public opposition to the invasion. Soon afterwards, the Royal Marines were moved to a C-130 Hercules transport aircraft, which would take them to Comodoro Rivadavia, where they were to be picked up by another airliner to Uruguay and on to the United Kingdom. Members of FIDF were not taken to Argentina along with members of NP 8901; instead they were disarmed and returned to their homes. As the Marines were being taken to Montevideo, one of them said to an Argentine guard "don't make yourself too comfy here mate, we'll be back".

Corporal York's section remained at large. On 4 April, they reached a secluded shepherd's hut owned by a Mrs Watson. York had no radio, and due to worries about possible civilian deaths chose to surrender to Argentine forces. They gave their position to the Argentine Army using a local islander's radio, and York subsequently ordered his men to destroy and then bury their weapons.

In Buenos Aires, huge flag-waving crowds flooded the Plaza de Mayo upon hearing the news. Argentina's losses in the operation were one dead and three wounded. In London, where the bad news was fully known from Argentine sources, the government was in a state of shock. The crisis prompted the resignation of the British Foreign Secretary, Lord Carrington.

The next day, Argentine forces captured the island chain of South Georgia, 1350 km to the east of the Falklands. In that action, the Argentines suffered one sailor from the corvette ARA *Guerrico* and two marines killed (Navy Corporal Patricio Guanca and marine conscripts Mario Almonacid and Jorge Aguila). One British Royal Marine was wounded in an exchange of fire with the Argentine troops. The Marines eventually surrender when his position was fired on by the *Guerrico's* 40 mm cannons.

Informing London

At 4.30pm on 2 April, the Governor's telex operator had this conversation

with a Ministry of Defence operative in London, announcing that the islands were under Argentine control.
LON (London): HELLO THERE WHAT ARE ALL THESE RUMOURS WE HEAR THIS IS LON
FK (Falklands): WE HAVE LOTS OF NEW FRIENDS
LON: WHAT ABOUT INVASION RUMOURS
FK: THOSE ARE THE FRIENDS I WAS MEANING
LON: THEY HAVE LANDED
FK: ABSOLUTELY
LON: ARE YOU OPEN FOR TRAFFIC IE NORMAL TELEX SERVICE
FK: NO ORDERS ON THAT YET ONE MUST OBEY ORDERS
LON: WHOSE ORDERS
FK: THE NEW GOVERNORS
LON: ARGENTINA
FK: YES
LON: ARE THE ARGENTINIANS IN CONTROL
FK: YES YOU CAN'T ARGUE WITH THOUSANDS OF TROOPS PLUS ENORMOUS NAVY SUPPORT WHEN YOU ARE ONLY 1600 STRONG. STAND BY.

Operation timeline

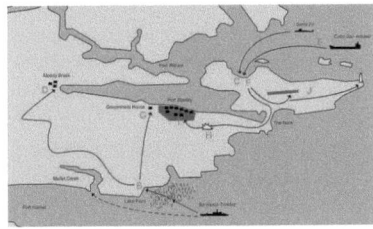

Operation *Rosario*

- **A.** 21:30 1 April – The Type 42 destroyer ARA *Santisima Trinidad* begins loading naval commandos of the Amphibious Commandos Group into 21 small inflatable motor boats. These set out for Mullet Creek but sail too far north and are caught up in beds of kelp, which cause problems for the boats. They decide to head for the nearest beach, which is near Lake Point.
- **B.** 23:00 1 April – The first group of 84 men lands on an unnamed beach at Lake Point. The group splits into a smaller force led by Lieutenant-Commander Giachino which heads towards Government House, and a larger force commanded by Lieutenant-Commander Sabarots which heads towards Moody Brook barracks.
- **C.** 04:30 2 April – A small advanced team of the Tactical Divers Group is landed undetected from the Submarine ARA *Santa Fe* near Yorke Bay.
- **D.** 05:30 2 April – Lieutenant-Commander Sabarots' force reaches and surrounds the barracks. They throw tear gas grenades into the buildings and storm the buildings with heavy machine gun fire. They find the buildings deserted.
- **E.** 06:00 2 April – 20 FMC Amtracs and several LARC-V stores-carrying vehicles land on Yorke Bay from the assault ship ARA *Cabo San Antonio*. The force splits into 3 groups:
  - A four Amtrac vanguard. Including one carrying the Army Platoon.
  - The main force of 14 Amtracs.
  - The second in command, a recovery Amtrac and LARC vehicles.
- **F.** 06:30 2 April – The first Amtracs meet no resistance. The Army platoon secures the deserted airport, previously swept by Navy tactical divers.
- **G.** 06:30 2 April – An Argentine force of 16 naval commandos reaches Government House, where they are stopped by 31 Royal Marines, 11 armed Royal Navy personnel and 1 local. Three Argentines are wounded, including the leader of the platoon, Lieutenant-Commander Giachino, who later dies. Another three are later captured inside the House, although by then (around 8:00) talks with Argentine officials about the surrender had already begun.
- **H.** 07:15 2 April – Having met no resistance, the Argentine Amtracs advance on Stanley, when they are ambushed from a house about 500 metres from the road. Royal Marines use rockets and machine guns. The Royal Marines fall back to government house. One of the Amtracs is scarred by machine gun fire, and there is one minor injury.
- **I.** 08:30 2 April – The Argentine Amtrac force secures Stanley.
- **J.** Lieutenant Colonel Seineldín's Regiment 25th platoon begin to clear the runway, while Navy tactical divers provide security on the airport and seize the lighthouse.

Reaction in the United Nations

On 3 April 1982 the United Nations Security Council comprising the 5 permanent members and the 10 elected members (Poland, Spain, Ireland, Panama, Guyana, Japan, Jordan, Uganda, Zaire, and Togo) passed the Resolution 502 demanding an immediate withdrawal of all Argentine forces from the islands and called on the governments of Argentina and the United Kingdom to seek a diplomatic solution to the situation and refrain from further military action. Panama voted against this resolution, with China, Poland, Spain and the USSR abstaining. All 10 remaining members voted for the resolution.

Source (edited): "http://en.wikipedia.org/wiki/1982_invasion_of_the_Falkland_Islands"

Invasion of South Georgia

The **Invasion of South Georgia** (Spanish: *Operación Georgias*), also known as the **Battle of Grytviken**, took place on 3 April 1982, when Argentine naval forces seized control of the east coast of South Georgia after overpowering a small group of Royal Marines at Grytviken. The Argentine intervention had begun on 19 March, when a group of civilian scrap metal workers illegally arrived at Leith Harbour on board the transport ship ARA *Bahía Buen Suceso* and raised the Argentine flag. The scrap workers had been infiltrated by Argentine marines posing as civilian scientists.

Prelude

Map of South Georgia

The only British presence at Leith on 19 March was an Antarctic Survey (BAS) team, whose leader, Trefor Edwards, handed a message from London to the commander of the *Buen Suceso*, captain Briatore, demanding the removal of the Argentine flag and the departure of the party. At the same time, the Argentine crew had to report to the top BAS commander in Grytviken, Steve Martin. Briatore replied that the mission had the approval of the British embassy in Buenos Aires. Eventually, the Argentine captain ordered the lowering of the flag, but failed to report to Grytviken. The BAS commander sent a message to the Governor of the Falkland Islands, Rex Hunt (South Georgia being run as a dependency of the Falklands). After consulting London, Hunt was instructed to dispatch HMS *Endurance* to South Georgia with a detachment of 22 Royal Marines.

ARA *Almirante Irízar*, the first Argentine Navy ship to arrive at Grytviken in December 1981

The reason for the landing of scrap metal workmen at Leith was a 1978 contract between an Argentine businessman, Constantino Davidoff, and the British company Christian Salvesen, for the scrapping of the abandoned whale factories and facilities on the island. Aware of the contract, the Argentine Navy conceived of a plan to hijack Davidoff's business in South Georgia, in order to establish an undercover base on the disputed territory. The action was code named *Operation Alpha*. There had been already two other Argentine trips to South Georgia: on December 1981, on board the Argentine icebreaker ARA *Almirante Irízar*, when Davidoff made an inventory of the facilities; and on February 1982, when an alleged commercial rival of Davidoff, bank employee Adrian Marchessi, made an unannounced visit to Leith. Marchessi assessed Leith facilities on board the Panamanian registered yacht *Caiman*, which had sailed out of Mar del Plata. He later reported himself to Grytviken, claiming that he was part of Davidoff's scheme and giving the British authorities details of the December inspection and even of early Argentine trips during the 1970s.

The failure of the Argentines to comply with the diplomatic formalities prompted Whitehall to opt for a small-scale intervention. In the meantime, a formal protest was issued by the British embassy in Buenos Aires. The Argentine Foreign Minister's response appeared to defuse the crisis; the note asserted that the *Buen Suceso* would soon be leaving, and that the mission had no official sanction at all. By the morning of 22 March the *Buen Suceso* left Leith harbour. However, in the afternoon, a BAS observation post detected the presence of Argentine personnel and passed the information to London. In consequence, the Foreign Office chose to order HMS *Endurance* to evacuate any Argentine personnel remaining in South Georgia.

HMS *Endurance* at Mar del Plata naval base, during her trip to the Falklands in February 1982

The British moves met with a series of Argentine countermeasures: the corvettes ARA *Drummond* and ARA *Granville* were deployed between the Falklands and South Georgia, which would have allowed them to intercept the *Endurance* and remove any Argentine personnel on board. In addition, upon arrival at Leith, HMS *Endurance* found the Antarctic Survey ship ARA *Bahía Paraiso* at anchor. This vessel landed a party of 10 naval commandos picked up from South Orkney Islands. Facing a potential military showdown, the Foreign Office sought some sort of compromise. Lord Carrington proposed to his counterpart, Nicanor Costa Méndez, to indulge the workers presence at Leith, given the proper documentation, which could include the stamping of temporary permissions instead of passports, a concession crucial to the Argentine position. The Argentine intention, however, was that the arrival of any of its citizens to South Georgia should follow the procedures agreed on the communications treaty of 1971. Governor Rex Hunt strongly rejected this extension of the agreement, valid only for the Falklands jurisdiction, and raised his concerns to the British Government. Costa Mendez left things in a limbo; both countries were then on the brink of a major conflict.

Battle

2 April

Shortly before the Argentine landings on the Falklands, the *Bahía Paraíso* and the *Endurance* were playing a cat-and-mouse game around South Georgia, until 31 March, when the ships lost track of each other. The British plan was that Martin would be in charge until the Argentine forces showed any hostile intentions. If that occurred, Acting Lieutenant Keith Mills, the most senior officer of the Royal Marines party, would take command. On 2 April, Captain Alfredo Astiz, a veteran of the Dirty War whose extradition was requested by France for human rights violations, announced to the Argentine party in Leith that Argentina had taken over the Falklands. Meanwhile, the Argentine navy ordered the corvette ARA *Guerrico* to join the *Bahía Paraíso*, equipped with two helicopters (an Army Puma and a navy Alouette III) and carrying 40 marines, along with Astiz team at Leith. The aim was the capture of Grytviken. The group would be called *Grupo de Tareas 60.1* (Task Force 60.1), under the command of Captain Trombetta, on board *Bahía Paraíso*.

After learning of the fall of Stanley, Mills took urgent measures: his men fortified the beach at King Edward Point, near the entrance of the bay with wire and landmines, and prepared defences around the BAS buildings. The *Endurance*, some miles offshore, would provide communication between the small British detachment and London. The new rules of engagement authorized Mills to "fire in self defence, after warning". A later statement from the British government instructed the marines to "not resist beyond the point where lives might be lost to no avail." On the other side, the Argentine plans for 2 April in South Georgia were thwarted by poor weather. These plans consisted in the landing of Astiz's special forces on Hope Point, near Grytviken, to secure the arrival of the bulk of the land forces, carried by helicopter. The *Guerrico* would provide naval fire support outside the bay. But the arrival of the corvette was delayed by a storm, so a new course of action was decided for the next day. According to the new plan, the first landing would be led by *Guerrico*'s Alouette helicopter, followed by three waves of marines on a Puma from *Bahía Paraíso*. After sending a radio message demanding the British surrender, Trombetta would order the *Guerrico* to make a thrust into Grytviken harbor, right in front of King Edward point. The Argentine rules of engagement authorized the corvette to fire her weapons only at request of the landing parties. Astiz's men would remain in the rearguard on board the *Bahía Paraíso*. All the forces involved should avoid enemy casualties as long as possible. Freedman believes that Trombetta made these provisions thinking he was dealing only with the BAS team.

3 April

At 7:30 A.M., as the weather improved, *Bahia Paraiso* demanded the surrender of Grytviken. The message intimated that Rex Hunt had surrendered not only the Falklands, but also its dependencies, which was untrue. Lt Mills copied and forwarded the message to HMS *Endurance*, with the intention of buying time. At the same time, he invited the BAS personnel to take cover inside the local church. By then, the Alouette was overflying Grytviken and the *Guerrico* was making her first entrance into the cove. According to Mayorga, Captain Carlos Alfonso, commander of the *Guerrico*, hesitated whether or not to expose the corvette in such narrow waters. Mayorga also supports Freedman's speculation about Trombetta's wrong assumptions regarding British military presence around the harbour, citing an official report. Trombetta also had some reservations about the combat readiness of the warship since she had been in dry dock just days before departing from her home base at Puerto Belgrano.

Helicopter shot down

1999 remains of the Argentine Puma helicopter, shot down during the invasion

The Puma landed a first group of 15 Argentine marines on King Edward point at 11:41 AM, on the opposite side from Shackleton House, where the Royal Marines were entrenched. By then, the *Guerrico* knew that the general area of deployment of the Royal Marines was on the northern shore of the cove's mouth. The second wave of marines took off from *Bahia Paraiso* deck on board the Puma at 11:47. The commander of the Argentine group already inland, Lt Luna, requested via the *Guerrico*—he had no direct communication with *Bahia Paraiso*—that the second wave should be equipped with 60 mm mortars, but the party was already in flight. The landing was to take place to the east of Luna's position, well within the view of the British detachment. The helicopter was spotted by Mills and his men and met by intense automatic fire. The pilot was able to cross the bay and crash-landed the helicopter on the southern bank of the bay. Two men were killed and four wounded. At the same time, Luna's troops started their march towards Shackleton House, but the marines pinned them down with heavy gunfire. Therefore, Luna asked the *Guerrico* for fire support.

ARA *Guerrico*

Aft view of ARA *Guerrico* showing her 40 mm twin guns right after the battle of Grytviken

The corvette then carried out her second thrust into the cove, and at 11:55 opened fire. To her commander's disappointment, the 20 mm guns jammed after the first shot, and the 40 mm mounting after firing just six rounds. The 100 mm gun became useless after the first shot. Completely exposed, the warship had no other choice but to go ahead in order to put about. At 11:59, the corvette was hit by small arms fire and 84 mm *Carl Gustav* anti-tank shells. According to Mills, his party opened fire from a distance of 550 meters. The shooting killed one seaman and injured five others, damaging electrical cables, the 40 mm gun, one Exocet launcher and the 100 mm mounting. All Argentine sources acknowledge that more than 200 small arms rounds hit the corvette. In the meantime, Lt Busson's Alouette had been ferrying more Argentine Marines ashore, out of range of the British weapons. While the battered *Guerrico* steered out of the bay, the Argentine troops resumed the exchange of fire with Mills' marines. One of them was hit on his arm. Once she was out of range, *Guerrico* reopened fire with her 40 mm guns, now back in service. This convinced Mills that things were over, and he ordered his marines to cease fire. This happened at 12:48 according to Mayorga. Mills approached the Argentine positions waving a white coat, and surrendered,"after achieving his aim of compelling the Argentine troops to use military force". Mills and his men were taken in custody by Astiz's group, who had been left in reserve during the battle. HMS *Endurance* dispatched one of her *Wasp* helicopters to Cumberland Bay. The aircraft landed there, and spotted an Argentine corvette and a transport ship inside the cove, but found no signs of fighting. The *Endurance* remained in South Georgia waters until 5 April.

Aftermath

The corvette *Guerrico*, which had lost 50% of her firepower due to combat damage, left Grytviken along with *Bahia Paraiso* at 3:15 of 4 April, bound for Rio Grande. She spent three days in dry dock for repairs. The marines were disarmed and taken on board the *Bahia Paraiso*, ferried to Rio Grande and then airlifted to Montevideo. They eventually returned to the United Kingdom on 20 April. Some British BAS members working in remote areas continued their activities undeterred until the British reconquest. Wildlife film maker Cindy Buxton and her assistant were evacuated by a helicopter from HMS Endurance on 30 April. The Argentine Navy left a detachment of 55 marines on the island. The 39 scrap metal workers also remained in Leith. South Georgia was retaken by British forces on 25 April 1982, during Operation Paraquat.

Decorations and honours

- Lieutenant Mills and Lieutenant Commander John Anthony Ellerbeck (who commanded *Endurance*'s helicopters) were awarded the Distinguished Service Cross.
- Sergeant Peter James Leach, RM, was awarded the Distinguished Service Medal.
- Captain Nick Barker, HMS *Endurance*'s captain, was appointed Commander of the Order of the British Empire.
- Principal Corporal (Gunnery) Francisco Solano Paez was awarded La Nacion Argentina al Valor en Combate.

Source (edited): "http://en.wikipedia.org/wiki/Invasion_of_South_Georgia"

Operation Algeciras

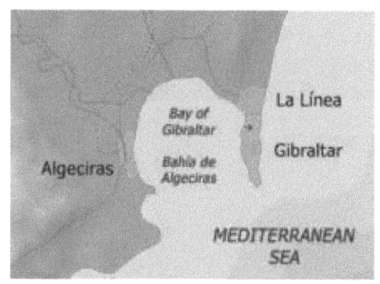

Map of the Bay of Gibraltar.

Operation Algeciras was an ill-fated Argentine plan to sabotage a Royal Navy warship in Gibraltar during the Falklands War. The premise being that if the British military felt vulnerable in Europe, they would decide to keep some vessels in Europe rather than send them to the Falklands.

A commando team observed British naval traffic in the area from Spain during 1982, waiting to attack a target of opportunity when ordered, using frogmen and Italian limpet mines.

The plan was to launch divers from Algeciras, have them swim across the bay, to Gibraltar, under cover of darkness, attach the mines to a British naval ship and swim back to Algeciras. The timed detonators would cause the mines to explode after the divers had time to safely swim back across the bay. The plan was foiled when the Spanish police became suspicious of their behavior and arrested them before any attack could be mounted.

Planning and participants

The operation was conceived, ordered

and directly managed by Admiral Jorge Anaya, who at the time, was a member of the governing Galtieri junta and head of the Argentine Navy in 1982. The plan was top secret and not shared with other members of the government. Anaya summoned to his office Admiral Eduardo Morris Girling, who was responsible for the Naval Intelligence Service, and explained to him the convenience of hitting the Royal Navy in Europe. Girling would be the one who would make the plan and select the participants but Anaya remained in charge of the operation throughout.

Striking in the United Kingdom was considered at first but it was thought that the commandos would have difficulty remaining unnoticed and Spain was chosen because the commandos could more easily pass unnoticed as tourists.

The leader of the operation was Héctor Rosales, a spy and former naval officer. He was in charge but would not participate in the actual placing of the mines which was left to the experts.

Three former members of the Peronist guerrilla Montoneros were convinced to participate in spite of the earlier repression of the Montoneros by the military.

The leader of the commandos was Máximo Nicoletti, a diver and expert in underwater explosives. His father served in the Italian navy's underwater demolition team during the Second World War and now owned a diving business. In the early 70's Nicoletti had joined the Montoneros and engaged in urban actions labelled terrorist by the military junta. On 1 November 1974 Nicoletti placed a remote-controlled bomb under the yacht of the police chief of the Argentine Federal Police, Alberto Villar, who was killed together with his wife. On 22 September 1975, while the destroyer ARA Santísima Trinidad was still under construction in Buenos Aires, Nicoletti placed an explosive charge under the hull which caused it to sink.

Later in the decade, Nicoletti was arrested by the infamous Grupo de Tareas 33/2 of the Escuela de Mecánica de la Armada (ESMA) but escaped serious punishment by cooperating with the authorities.

Soon, due to his cooperation and expertise, he managed to get himself appointed to carry out a similar submarine attack against a Chilean ship because tensions between Chile and Argentina were high due to the Beagle Channel dispute. This attack was not carried out in the end because the disagreement between Chile and Argentina was finally resolved peacefully. Nicoletti was then sent to Venezuela as a spy but he was discovered and had to return to Argentina. Shortly after he settled in Miami, but when he heard of the Argentine invasion of the Falkland Islands he immediately got in touch with the Argentinean government in case his services were needed and he was instructed to return to Buenos Aires.

The other two commandos, both also ex-Montoneros, were Antonio Nelson Latorre, nicknamed "Diego, el Pelado" (or "el Pelado Diego") and another man who went by "Marciano" and who has remained anonymous to this day. Both had participated with Nicoletti in earlier sabotage plans.

In the event of capture, Argentina would deny all knowledge. The agents were to say they were Argentine patriots acting on their own. They had orders not to do anything which could involve or embarrass Spain, to sink a British naval vessel and to get express approval from Anaya before carrying out any attack.

When planning the operation in Argentina it was decided that acquiring or manufacturing explosives in Spain would prove too difficult and so two explosive mines with timed detonators would be shipped to Spain via diplomatic pouch and would be delivered to the commando in Spain. Italian limpet mines were acquired for this purpose and shipped to Spain in diplomatic pouch as planned.

Situation in Spain at the time

At that time the political climate in Spain was unstable with the government of Leopoldo Calvo Sotelo having political difficulties on many fronts, including with the military who distrusted him. The trials for those responsible for the military coup attempt of 23-F a year earlier were concluding and this further raised tensions. The Basque group ETA were very active and police controls on roads were common. The upcoming 1982 FIFA World Cup in Spain meant the police were very alert to any suspicious or terrorist activity. The police requested that everybody remain vigilant, and that people should report anything unusual, especially within the travel industry.

Execution

The commandos were issued counterfeit Argentine passports under false names and marked with false earlier entry stamps to Spain. This was done so the Argentine government could deny any involvement in case the commandos were discovered and the passports were made by another ex-montonero, Victor Basterra.

On 24 April Nicoletti and Latorre left Buenos Aires for Paris where Latorre's passport raised the suspicions of French authorities but they were finally allowed to continue their onward travel by air to Malaga. They carried the closed-circuit, military scuba gear in their luggage and passed customs without raising suspicion. They carried plenty of cash in US dollars and would pay for all their expenses and purchases in cash.

They both checked in to a hotel in Estepona and spent some days surveying the area after which they travelled to Madrid in a rented car to meet Rosales and Marciano. They then rented another two cars in Madrid and went to the office of the Argentine Naval Attaché to pick up the mines. While in Spain the commando communicated daily by telephone with the Naval Attaché of the Argentine Embassy in Madrid, who would, in turn, communicate with his superiors in Buenos Aires.

The commando of four, travelling in three cars, travelled south using main roads. The mines were carried in the trunk of a car, in a bag and by the shape and appearance would be immediately discovered to be explosives by anyone who saw them. While cover stories could be plausibly invented for the specialized military scuba gear, there was no way to explain the explosives so they had to be careful that they were not stopped at any police control.

They travelled to the south of Spain separately, with Nicoletti going ahead as a scout and the other two cars ten minutes apart each. They had no way to communicate between cars except visually. Nicoletti did come up to a police block and turned around to warn his accomplices but even though he saw them and signaled the first car behind him did not see him and continued until it too saw the police control and turned around. They all met again, their U-turns having gone unnoticed. They then decided to continue south using minor routes.

When they arrived in the area near Algeciras they checked separately into three different hotels and would change hotels often over the next few weeks. They would renew their rentals on a weekly basis and always pay cash for everything, which eventually raised suspicions and lead to their arrest. They kept the explosives in one of the cars and used only the other two for transport.

During the first days they surveyed the Algeciras bay in search of the best place to enter the water and to observe the nautical traffic in and out of the port of Gibraltar. They observed that there was not as much surveillance at Gibraltar as they had expected. Two sentry observation posts were unmanned and only a navy vessel cruised the area around the port.

They bought an inflatable raft, telescope and fishing tackle to give cover to their activities and the raft to be used to cross the bay part of the way. The plan was to enter the water at about 6 PM, swim across, plant the mines at about midnight, swim back, exit at about 5 AM and the mines would explode shortly after.

They would then drive north to Barcelona, cross into France, then Italy and, from there, fly back to Argentina.

The first opportunity came when a British minesweeper entered Gibraltar but Anaya denied his permission to proceed on account that he thought the target was not worth the effort and it was better to wait for a bigger ship. A few days later a large oil tanker with non-British flag presented itself as a possible target. Nicoletti suggested sinking it would block the port of Gibraltar for a long time but Anaya refused permission in case it caused an oil spill and environmental disaster that would harm and outrage Spain and possibly affect other Mediterranean countries.

Over the weeks the commandos continued their routine of changing hotels and renewing their car rental. During this time the British task force was already sailing south towards the Falklands.

Finally, a high-value target, the frigate HMS Ariadne, arrived at Gibraltar on May 2, but Anaya again refused permission, this time because the President of Peru, Fernando Belaúnde, had just produced a comprehensive peace plan and Anaya believed this might produce a peaceful resolution, which could only be undermined by a successful attack in Gibraltar.

But the same day, May 2, the Argentine cruiser ARA General Belgrano was sunk by the British nuclear attack submarine HMS *Conqueror* which meant war was now inevitable.

The following day, May 3, Nicoletti anticipated that permission would now be given by Anaya and, because hostilities had broken out, he asked if the team could claim to be acting for the Argentine military if they were caught. This was refused but they were ordered to execute the plan.

Failure

The following day Nicoletti slept late, as he usually did because the plan was to act at night, while Latorre and Rosales went to the car rental agency to extend the rental for another week. The owner of the rental business, Manuel Rojas, had become suspicious on previous encounters. He noticed that the man had keys with him for cars rented in other car rental businesses, that he always paid in cash using American dollars and that he never came in exactly when he said he would but rather would come in earlier or later. Because of this he had notified the police who asked him to call them next time the man came by and to try to keep him there until they arrived. This he did and the men were arrested. The police then went to arrest the other two men and they found Nicoletti and Marciano still asleep. The police initially thought they had a gang of common criminals but, in spite of the orders to the contrary, Nicoletti soon declared that they were Argentine agents.

Miguel Catalán was the police chief in Málaga at the time and the minister of the interior, Juan Jose Rosón, instructed him to keep the arrests secret. The Spanish government decided to expel the four men without penalty or prosecution and did not want any publicity.

The police were told to take the arrested men to Málaga. Nicoletti, in the documentary says once the policemen realized they were not common criminals their attitude changed and became more favorable. The police let Nicoletti handle the explosives as he had training the police did not have. Then Nicoletti proposed inviting them to lunch and the police accepted so the police convoy (carrying the explosives) stopped for lunch at a roadside restaurant. Then they went to pick up some clothes at a dry cleaners and finally headed for the Málaga police headquarters.

By coincidence, the president of the government Leopoldo Calvo Sotelo, was campaigning in Malaga and ordered that the men be quietly taken to Madrid in an airplane which had been chartered for the campaign. The men were not interrogated or put on trial. They were quietly flown to Madrid in police custody, from there were flown to the Canary Islands, also with police custody, and finally were put on a flight to Buenos Aires without custody. They were returned under the same passports, now known to be false. Spain had recently joined NATO and Sotelo preferred to not create tensions with the

UK or with Argentina and quietly returning the men to Argentina seemed like the best course.

The operation was handled entirely by the Spanish Police and the Ministry of the Interior while the CESID (Spanish military intelligence agency) was not informed or involved. The operation was kept secret by all and was not openly talked about or disclosed by the participants until many years later. The Spanish police were ordered to destroy all associated records. At the last minute, at the airport, the police chief realized they had not taken ID information of the men and called to give order that photos of the men be taken. At the airport the police charged with taking the photos thought it would look awkward to take ID photos in public and so a friendly, group photo of the commandos with the police guarding them was taken. This photo has not been found.

An article published by The Sunday Times in October 1983 titled *How Argentina tried to blow up the Rock* exposes the basic plot but contains many errors because little was known about the operation at that time.

Argentine writer Juan Luis Gallardo wrote a novel based on this operation, *Operación Algeciras*.

In 2003 a documentary was made where Anaya, Nicoletti and other participants were interviewed. Nigel West, a British writer who specialises in covert operations, told the documentary team that Britain had known about the plot because of telephone-taps of conversations between Argentina's embassy in Madrid and Buenos Aires, but this seems unlikely because if that were the case it would have been the military intelligence who would have intervened. It seems much more likely that, as Nicoletti and others claim in the documentary, the Spanish police became suspicious due to the information supplied by the car rental agency and the Spanish police initially really had no idea that they had caught a military commando.

Source (edited): "http://en.wikipedia.org/wiki/Operation_Algeciras"

Operation Black Buck

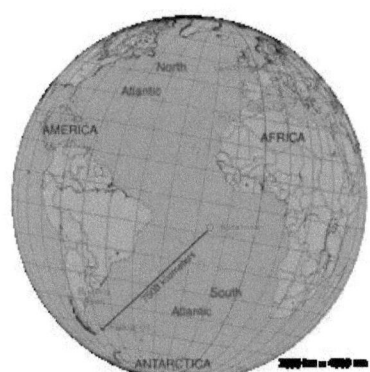

Operation Black Buck on the map

During the Falklands War, **Operations Black Buck 1** to **Black Buck 7** were a series of seven extremely long-range ground attack missions by Royal Air Force Vulcan bombers planned against Argentine positions in the Falkland Islands. Of the seven planned missions, only five were actually flown.

The Operation Black Buck raids comprised a series of five attacks on the Islands by RAF Avro Vulcan bombers of 44 Squadron, staged from RAF Ascension Island, close to the equator. The aircraft carried either twenty-one 1,000 lb bombs internally or two or four Shrike anti-radar missiles externally. The overall effect of the raids on the war is difficult to determine, and the raids consumed precious tanker resources. The raids did minimal damage to the runway and damage to radars was quickly repaired. Commonly dismissed as post-war propaganda, Argentine sources originally claimed that the Vulcan raids influenced Argentina to withdraw some of the Mirage IIIs from the Southern Argentina Defence Zone to the Buenos Aires Defence Zone. This dissuasive effect was however watered down when British officials made clear that there would be no strikes on air bases in Argentina. It has been suggested that the Black Buck raids were pressed home by the Royal Air Force because the British armed forces had been cut in the late seventies and the RAF may have desired a greater role in the conflict to prevent further cuts. A single crater was produced on the runway, rendering it impossible for the airfield to be used by fast jets. Argentine ground crew repaired the runway within twenty-four hours, but only to a level of quality suitable for the C-130 Hercules and Aermacchi MB-339 jets. Many sources claim that fake craters confounded British damage assessment, however, the British were well aware that the runway remained in use by C-130 and IA 58 Pucara aircraft.

The Vulcan lacked the range to fly to the Falklands without refuelling several times, as it had been designed for medium-range stand-off nuclear missions in Europe. The RAF's tanker planes were mostly converted Handley Page Victor bombers with similar range, so they too had to be refuelled in the air. Thus, a total of 11 tankers were required for only two Vulcans, a huge logistical effort, given that both the tankers and bombers had to use the same strip.

The raids, at almost 8,000 nautical miles (15,000 km) and 16 hours for the return journey, were the longest-ranged bombing raids in history at that time (surpassed in the Gulf War of 1991 by USAF Boeing B-52G Stratofortresses flying from the continental United States but using forward-positioned tankers).

Of the five Black Buck raids, three were against Stanley Airfield, with the other two anti-radar missions using Shrike anti-radiation missiles.

Background

Vulcan over Ascension Island on 18 May 1982

Without aircraft able to cover the long distance, activities in the South Atlantic would be carried out by the Royal Navy and the British Army. Plans were set in motion within the RAF to see if it could carry out any operations near the Falklands.

The airfield nearest to the Falklands and usable for RAF operations was on Ascension Island, a British territory with a single runway at Wideawake airfield which was leased to the US.

Long-range operations were entirely dependent on the RAF's tanker fleet and so Handley Page Victor tankers were transferred from RAF Marham to Ascension Island. The RAF tankers were capable of being refuelled in flight, which meant that it was possible to set up relays of aircraft.

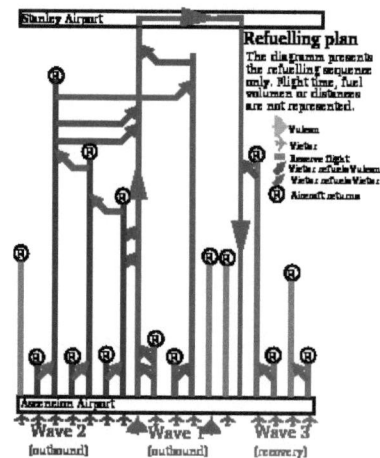

The attacking Vulcan was refueled seven times on the outward journey and once on the return journey.

The Avro Vulcan was the last of the British V-bombers in operational use for bombing but their squadrons were to be disbanded imminently. They were based in the UK and assigned to NATO for nuclear operations; neither air-to-air refuelling nor conventional bombing had been practised for several years.

At Marham the tanker force was set to planning refuelling operations to take one or more bombers to the Falklands and back. At RAF Waddington, the retraining of crews in conventional bombing and in-flight refuelling was begun. Aircraft were selected based upon their engines; only those with the more powerful Bristol Olympus 301 engines were considered suitable. One of the most challenging tasks was reinstating the refuelling system, which had been blocked off.

One Victor was converted into an improvised photo-reconnaissance aircraft. Victors arrived at Ascension Island on 18 April.

Three 22-year-old Vulcan B2s drawn from No. 44, 50 and No. 101 Squadron RAF were deployed to Wideawake airfield on Ascension Island. Squadron Leader Neil McDougall, Squadron Leader John Reeve and Flight Lieutenant Martin Withers captained the Vulcans.

To give improved electronic countermeasures (ECM) against Argentine defences which were known to include Tigercat missile and radar-controlled anti-aircraft guns, Dash 10 pods from Blackburn Buccaneer aircraft at RAF Honington were fitted to the wings on improvised pylons. To navigate across the featureless seas, inertial guidance systems were borrowed from VC-10s and two installed in each Vulcan.

The wet wings could contain 9,200 gal (41,823 litres) and based on estimates of their fuel need eleven Victor tankers, including two standby aircraft, were assigned to refuel the Vulcans before and after their attacks on the Falklands. The attacking Vulcan was refueled seven times on the outward journey and once on the return journey, using over 220,000 gallons of aviation fuel during the mission. Each aircraft carried either twenty-one 1,000-pound (450 kg) bombs or four Shrike anti-radar missiles (Dash 10 pod) with three 1,000 gal (4,546 litres) auxiliary fuel tanks in the bomb bay. The bombs were intended to cause damage to Argentine installations, especially Port Stanley Airport; it was hoped that the attacks would cause the defenders to switch on defensive radars, which would then be targeted by the missiles. The lighter Shrike-armed Vulcans could loiter in the area longer than the bomb-armed Vulcans.

Missions

Black Buck One

XM607, the first Vulcan to participate in Black Buck

The first surprise attack on the islands, on 30 April-1 May was aimed at the main runway at Port Stanley Airport. Carrying twenty-one 1,000 lbs general-purpose bombs, the bomber was to fly across the line of the runway at about 35 degrees. The bomb release system was timed to drop sequentially from 10,000 ft so that at least one bomb would land on the runway.

For the mission, two Vulcans took off from RAF Ascension Island; XM598 was the lead with XM607 as the reserve. Shortly after take off, XM598, commanded by Squadron Leader John Reeve, suffered a pressurisation failure (a rubber seal on the "Direct Vision" side window had perished) and was forced to return to Ascension. XM607, captained by Flight Lieutenant Martin Withers, took over.

As well as XM598, one of the Victor tankers returned to Ascension with a faulty refuelling hose system and its place was taken by a reserve.

The Vulcan was over its normal maximum take-off weight - each carried, as well as extra equipment like the DASH 10 and a chemical toilet, a highly experienced Air to Air Refuelling Instructor (AARI) from the Victor tanker force who would fly the Vulcan during refuelling - and fuel usage was higher than expected. As a result of the fuel demand and problems in flight with refuelling, two of the Victors had to fly further south than planned, eating into their own reserves, and one of these the last Victor to refuel the Vulcan was past the last refuelling bracket before turning home. Both Victors would need tankers sent south to refuel them so they could reach Ascension.

XM607 made the final approach at around 300 ft above the sea. Before climbing to attack height the H2S radar was successfully locked on to offset markers on the coast and bombing handed over to the control system. The attack was delivered around 4 am local time.

Control tower of Stanley airport shortly after operation Black Buck I

XM607 then climbed away from the airfield and headed nearly due north to a planned rendezvous with a Victor some way off the coast of Rio de Janeiro. As it passed the British Task Force it signalled "superfuse" indicating a successful attack. Its journey continued up within range of the South American coast to its rendezvous with a tanker. After contacting control with an update, the tanker was sent further south. To help bring the two planes together a Nimrod Maritime Reconnaissance aircraft was flown from Wideawake to the area. Without an in-flight refuelling system it was unable to loiter long. XM607 made the link and was able to return to Ascension.

Northwood received the superfuse message by 8:30 and the MoD shortly thereafter. The news of the bombing raid was reported on the BBC World Service before either the Vulcan or the last tanker arrived at Ascension.

The stick of twenty-one 1000 lb bombs crossed the airfield, damaged the airport tower, scored a single direct hit in the centre of the runway and killed two Air Force personnel. However, it still remained operational for the Argentine C-130 Hercules transports. The bombs falling on either side of the runway caused slight damage to tented installations in the airfield perimeter. This was due to the careful dispersal of equipment by the base commander.

The attack took the Argentines (as well as the rest of the world) completely by surprise.

Withers was awarded the Distinguished Flying Cross for his part in the action. Tuxford who had piloted the last Victor to refuel XM607, received the Air Force Cross.

Black Buck Two

During the night of 3 May-4 May, XM607 (flown by Squadron Leader John Reeve and his crew of No 50 Squadron) flew a near identical mission to the first. XM598 acted as flying reserve aircraft. This raid targeted the area at the western end of the runway. According to RAF and White's book this was intended to prevent Argentine engineers from extending the runway sufficiently to make it capable of accommodating high performance combat aircraft. However according to the historian Lawrence Freedman BB2 missed the runway because of the presence of Argentine Roland SAM. Two Argentine soldiers were wounded according to Argentine sources, which also confirm impacts near the western end of the airstrip.

Black Buck Three

This mission, scheduled for 13 May, was scrubbed before take-off due to strong headwinds. Vulcans XM612 and XM607.

Black Buck Four

An AGM-45 Shrike anti-radiation missile on a trolley

This mission with XM597, scheduled for 28 May, was also scrubbed, but only some 5 hours after the Vulcan had taken off. One of the supporting Victor aircraft, which were flying refuelling operations, suffered a failure of their hose-and-drogue refuelling unit, and the flight had to be recalled. XM598 acted as flying reserve aircraft.

The mission had been due to be the

first using American supplied AGM-45 Shrike Anti-Radar missiles, which were mounted to the Vulcans using improvised underwing pylons.

Black Buck Five

XM597, showing mission markings from its two Black Buck missions and Brazilian internment.

This mission, flown by Squadron Leader Neil McDougall and his crew from 50 Squadron in XM597, on 31 May, was the first successful anti-radar mission equipped with AGM-45A Shrike missiles. The main target was a Westinghouse AN/TPS-43 long range 3D radar that the Argentine Air Force deployed during April to guard the airspace surrounding the Falklands. In order for the missiles to work the targeted radar had to transmit up until the missiles impacted. The first missile impacted 10 metres away from the target, causing minor blast damage to the wave-guide assembly, but not disabling the radar. Fearing further attack, the Argentine operators used the simple counter-measure of turning their radar off preventing further damage. The AN/TPS-43 radar remained operational during the rest of the conflict. XM598 acted as flying reserve aircraft.

Black Buck Six

The Skyguard radar destroyed by Black Buck Six

This mission, again flown by Squadron Leader Neil McDougall in XM597, attacked and destroyed a Skyguard fire-control radar of the army's 601 Anti-aircraft battalion on 3 June, killing 4 radar operators: an officer, a sergeant and two soldiers. On its return flight, the aircraft was forced to divert to Rio de Janeiro in Brazil after its in-flight refuelling probe broke. One of the missiles it was carrying was ditched into the ocean to reduce drag, but the other remained stuck on the pylon and could not be released. Sensitive documents containing classified information were jettisoned into the sea via the crew hatch, and a "Mayday" signal was sent. The aircraft was cleared to land by Brazilian authorities with less than 2,000 lbs of fuel remaining. This was insufficient to have completed a circuit of the airport. The aircraft was interned for nine days at Galeão Air Force Base, before the crew and aircraft were returned on 11 June, after both had been treated well by the authorities. However, the remaining Shrike missile was confiscated and never returned. XM598 acted as flying reserve aircraft.

Black Buck Seven

The final Black Buck mission (XM607 flown by Flight Lieutenant Martin Withers) was against Argentine troop positions close to Stanley on 12 June, successfully cratering the eastern end of the airfield and causing widespread damage to airfield stores and facilities. However the bombs were supposed to detonate in mid-air, not to explode at impact. Since the bomb raid was conducted so late in the war the RAF wouldn't risk damaging the runway. The runway would be important for RAF Phantom FGR.2 operations when the Falklands Islands were British again. The Argentine ground forces surrendered two days later. XM598 acted as flying reserve aircraft.

Effect

Aerial reconnaissance photo of Port Stanley Airport. The craters from Black Buck One's bombs can be seen in the middle. Black Buck Two's craters can be seen more clearly to the left.

The military success of *Black Buck* remains controversial to this day with some independent sources describing it as minimal, the damage to the airfield and radars being quickly repaired. The runway continued to be used by Argentine C-130s until the end of the war and was also available for Aermacchi MB-339 jets and FMA Pucarás. As a result of the controversy a number of common misconceptions exist about the raid.

Although commonly dismissed as British propaganda, Argentine sources confirm claims that *Black Buck* was initially responsible for the withdrawal of a number of Mirage IIIEA from operations over the islands in order to protect the mainland. This dissuasive effect was however watered down when British officials made clear that there would not be strikes on air bases in Argentina.

There are urban legends that claim Argentine engineers building the runway plotted its position incorrectly on maps, leading to the British missing the runway. The runway at Port Stanley was in fact built by British engineers, replacing an earlier temporary strip constructed by LADE in the early 1970s.

The purposes of the raid and its impact on the runway are also commonly misunderstood. British air power doctrine recognises that attacks against the operating surfaces of runways can have limited effect. Planning for the raid called for a bomb run in a 35° cut across the runway, with the aim of placing at least one bomb on the runway and possibly two. The main purpose in doing so was to prevent the use of the runway by fast jets, in this respect the raid was successful as the repair to the runway was botched and subsequently there were several near accidents. However, it was realised at the time that the runway would likely remain open to use by C-130s; the RAF routinely practises rough field take offs in their C-130s.

The Argentines left the runway covered with piles of earth during the day, leading to claims this caused British intelligence to surmise that repairs were still in progress and misleading the British as to the condition of the airfield and the success of their raids. In fact, the British were well aware that C-130 flights continued to use the airfield and attempted to interdict these flights leading to the loss of a C-130 on 1 June, which was not, however, engaged in any resupply mission.

Another common misconception is that the Argentine forces made no attempt to use the airfield at Port Stanley as a base for high-performance jets. In early April the Argentine Naval Aviation installed arrestor gear on the runway to enable short landings and A-4Q Skyhawks of 3 Escuadrilla and S-2 Trackers (2-AS-22, 2-AS-25) deployed to the airfield performing several reconnaissance missions until April 13 when they were redeployed to the continent to embark on the *Veinticinco de Mayo*. After the carrier returned to port, and due the continuous naval bombardment of Stanley, the aircraft operated from Rio Grande, Tierra del Fuego and Río Gallegos, Santa Cruz respectively Engineers of the Argentine Air Force had added additional steel matting to extend the parking area for the Pucaras and Aermacchis that used the airfield but the main equipment to extend the runway was still on the ELMA cargo ship *Cordoba* which could not cross to the island due the British submarine threat

To the British, the raids achieved a number of non-material objectives. These included: demonstrating their willingness to defend British territories from forceful invasion, signalling British intent to recapture the Falklands and showing their ability to attack Argentine forces on the islands. It also demonstrated the possibility of escalating the conflict in future by striking industrial targets on the Argentine mainland. Regardless of whether or not the British actually intended to pursue these options and escalate the conflict, the Argentine leadership would have been fully aware of the implications.

According to Rowland White, the author of *Vulcan 607*, Vice Admiral Lombardo was led to believe that Black Buck One was the prelude to a full scale landing by the British. As a consequence, he ordered Rear Admiral Allara (commander of the Argentine carrier) to immediately attack the British fleet. This attack took the form of a pincer movement, the *General Belgrano* to the south and the *Veinticinco de Mayo* to the north. On 2 May, the *Belgrano* was sunk by the submarine HMS *Conqueror*, and after 368 of her crew lost their lives, the Argentine Navy withdrew to territorial waters and played no further part in the conflict.

At the time, it was the longest bombing raid in history, covering over 4,000 nautical miles (7,000 km), all of which were conducted over the open sea. This record was not broken until an American B-52 flew from the USA to Iraq, and then returned to RAF Mildenhall in England during Operation Desert Storm in 1991, although a major difference between the two was that the B-52s benefited from forward pre-positioned tankers for their aerial refuelling.

After the conflict ended, the runway was repaired and extended to allow the deployment of a detachment of Phantom FGR.2 fighters from No. 29 Squadron on 17 October 1982.
Source (edited): "http://en.wikipedia.org/wiki/Operation_Black_Buck"

Operation Corporate

Operation Corporate was the codename given to the 1982 British military involvement in the Falkland Islands during the Falklands War.

The 2 April 1982 Argentine invasion, Operation Rosario, took the British by surprise. The British undertook a series of military operations as a means of recapturing the Falklands from Argentine occupation.

The British counterinvasion was launched on 21 May, the capital city of Stanley fell on 14 June. On the British side 3 civilians and 255 service men were killed, and on the Argentine side 649 service men.
Source (edited): "http://en.wikipedia.org/wiki/Operation_Corporate"

Operation Keyhole

During Operation Corporate in the 1982 Falklands War, **Operation Keyhole** was a British special operation on Thule Island on the South Sandwich Islands. The Operation took place from 19-20 June 1982. 10 prisoners (one civilian and nine military personal) were evacuated to the tanker OLMEDA, accompanied by HMS YARMOUTH. They departed for South Georgia. The Argentine Base URUGUAY was closed and the buildings sealed to make them weatherproof. The other ships of Operation Keyhole (ENDURANCE, SALVAGEMAN) followed and were back at Cumberland East Bay/South Georgia by 24 June 1982. During the operation KEYHOLE nobody was killed or injured.

A Royal Marines team were landed on Thule Island covertly to observe Argentine activities. The harsh conditions on the island with an air temperature of minus 20 degrees Celsius and a gale gusting to sixty miles per hour, the chill factor caused an effective drop to minus fifty-two. Under the threat of the Royal Marines Party on the island and the ships cruising in front of the Argentine Base and several helicopters flying to the Argentine Base a white flag was raised. The ENDURANCE people who were forced to lower the Union Flag on South Georgia in 3 April hoisted now the Union Flag on Thule Island.

Source (edited): "http://en.wikipedia.org/wiki/Operation_Keyhole"

Operation Mikado

Argentine Navy Dassault-Breguet Super Étendard

Operation Mikado was the code name of a military plan by the United Kingdom to use Special Air Service troops to attack the home base of Argentina's five Etendard strike fighters at Río Grande, Tierra del Fuego during the 1982 Falklands War.

The aim of the operation was to destroy the Exocet missiles and the aircraft that carried them, and to kill the pilots in their quarters. Two plans were drafted and underwent preliminary rehearsal: a landing by approximately fifty-five SAS in two C-130 Hercules aircraft directly on the runway at Rio Grande; and infiltration of twenty-four SAS by inflatable boats brought within a few miles of the coast by the submarine HMS *Onyx*.

A helicopter reconnaissance mission on Río Grande was launched as a prelude to the main operation from HMS *Invincible* on 16 May, but after detecting an Argentine radar signal, the crew of the SH-3 Sea King and members of the SAS fled to Chile, where they destroyed their aircraft. According to Argentine sources, the helicopter was tracked by the radar of the destroyer ARA *Bouchard*, who sent a message to her sister ship ARA *Piedrabuena*, patrolling on the north, and then to the air base of Río Grande. Members of the Argentine 24th Regiment of Infantry claimed in 2007 that they hit the helicopter with small arms fire amid thick fog south of Rio Gallegos.

Neither of the proposed plans was implemented; the earlier airborne assault plan attracted considerable hostility from some members of the SAS, who considered the proposed raid a suicide mission. Ironically, the Rio Grande area would be defended by four full-strength battalions of Marine Infantry of the Argentine Marine Corps of the Argentine Navy, some of whose officers were trained in the UK by the SBS years earlier.

After the war, Argentine marine commanders admitted that they were waiting for some kind of landing by SAS forces but never expected a Hercules to land directly on their runways, although they would have pursued British forces even into Chilean territory in case of attack.

Source (edited): "http://en.wikipedia.org/wiki/Operation_Mikado"

Operation Paraquet

HMS *Antrim*

ARA *Santa Fe*

Operation Paraquet was the code name for the British military operation to recapture the Island of South Georgia from Argentine military control in April 1982 at the start of the Falklands War. The official name "Paraquet" is an alternative spelling of Parakeet, but the operation is perhaps more widely known as **Operation Paraquat**, an unofficial name adopted by troops in the South Atlantic who feared the operation would prove as lethal to them as the weedkiller Paraquat. This view prompted the exclamation *"kill Paraquat before it kills us."*

The operation, a subsidiary of the main Operation Corporate (recapture of the Falkland Islands from Argentina) was successful, leading to the island being restored to British rule on 25 April 1982.

Operation

The operation was ordered by Admiral Fieldhouse on 12 April 1982. It was to involve Mountain Troop from D Squadron SAS from Ascension Island, 150 Royal Marines on the tanker *Tidespring*, 2SBS on HMS *Plymouth* and 6SBS in the submarine HMS *Conqueror*. *Conqueror* was first on the scene and carried out a survey of key areas of the South Georgia coast. The operation was originally supposed to involve both SAS and SBS forces being infiltrated onto South Georgia by helicopters from the *Tidespring* and *Antrim*, but the plan had to be changed when the two Wessex helicopters transporting the SAS troops to an ambitious location on the northeast coast crashed in atrocious weather on Fortuna Glacier; the troops and aircrew were rescued by *Antrim*'s Wessex helicopter, the last remaining to the expedition.

On 9 April the submarine ARA *Santa Fe* left port in Argentina with a detachment of marines on board to reinforce the South Georgia garrison, and arrived safely in Grytviken on 24 April. However, on 25 April the *Santa Fe* was intercepted while sailing away and disabled by depth charges from Antrim's Wessex helicopter and subsequent attacks by task force Wasp and Lynx helicopters, which fired at least six AS-12 missiles on the submarine. The *Santa Fe* was forced to limp back to Grytviken.

There followed an immediate assault by an improvised group of Special Forces and Royal Marines, with two Royal Navy vessels (*Antrim* and *Plymouth*) conducting a naval bombardment demonstration on the low hills opposite Grytviken. The garrison at Grytviken and the crew of the disabled *Santa Fe* surrendered to M Company, 42 Commando, Royal Marines, after fifteen minutes at 17.15 GMT, although the garrison at Leith Harbour, under the command of Lieut. Commander Alfredo Astiz, surrendered the following day. Sweden and France requested Astiz extradition to the British authorities after learning about his capture, but his captors rejected the petition.

An Argentine prisoner of war, Navy Petty Officer Felix Artuso, a crewman of the *Santa Fe*, was mistakenly shot dead on April 26 after a British marine thought he was sabotaging the submarine and is buried at Grytviken Cemetery.

One of the most famous and legendary signals of the entire Falklands War was made by the British Landing Forces' commander Major Guy Sheridan RM after the surrender at Grytviken:

Be pleased to inform Her Majesty that the White Ensign flies alongside the Union Jack in South Georgia. God save the Queen.

Wildlife film maker Cindy Buxton and her assistant, who had been filming in an isolated part of the island before the invasion, were evacuated by a helicopter from HMS *Endurance* on 30 April.

Source (edited): "http://en.wikipedia.org/wiki/Operation_Paraquet"

Operation Sutton

During the 1982 Falklands War, **Operation Sutton** was the British landings on the shores of San Carlos Water, at Ajax Bay and Port San Carlos, near the San Carlos on East Falkland. During the night 3 Commando Brigade along with attached units of the Parachute Regiment were landed from the liner SS Canberra and the LPD HMS Fearless. There was very limited enemy resistance on the ground. However, an Argentinean Army platoon managed to shoot down two British Army Gazelle helicopters near Fanning Head before retreating north. As a result three Royal marines were killed in action. At least eight members of another platoon who fled the scene were left behind and captured by the British. Argentine commandos of the 601 Commando Company shot down a GR3 Harrier on a reconnaissance mission on Port Howard. The pilot, Flight Lieutenant Jerry Glover, bailed out and was taken prisoner. Six Argentine pilots were killed in the operation.

The invasion, part of the overall Operation Corporate, sparked a strong reply from the Argentine Air Force and the Argentine Naval Aviation which lead to the Battle of San Carlos.

Source (edited): "http://en.wikipedia.org/wiki/Operation_Sutton"